JAMES E. WARD JR.

ZERO VICTIM

OVERCOMING INJUSTICE WITH A NEW ATTITUDE

Second Paperback Edition

Cover design and photography by Charan Ingram

Published by Freiling Publishing, a division of Freiling Agency, LLC.

P.O. Box 1264,
Warrenton, VA 20188

www.FreilingPublishing.com

ISBN 978-0-692-29583-0

Printed in the United States of America

Dedication

To James Sr. (January 25, 1946-March 31, 2014), my beloved father, brother in Christ, and dear friend. There's not a day that goes by that I am not tempted to call or text you. You provided the seed for everything I could possibly do or become, so this book is for you. You have raised the standard for fatherhood for me and for many other men, by raising your son in such a way that he could one day humbly become your mentor and pastor.

I can only wish that you were here to read this book and then "preach" the message to your friends in the breakfast club as if it was your own. Your affirmation and words of encouragement caused me to at least believe that I was a good son, which was plenty enough for me to do my best to behave as though I was, in order to never disappoint you. You knew that high expectations create great men and you provided them for me.

Thank you for surrendering your life entirely to Christ and for faithfully loving Mom, Don, Kandys, Sharon, Hannah, Jonathan, and me unconditionally. I am eternally grateful to you. Until we meet again.

Table of Contents

Acknowledgments

No significant accomplishment can be achieved without the cooperation and sacrifice of many talented people. I am the product of the sum total of the investment of those around me. My relationships alone make me a very wealthy man!

To Sharon, my beautiful and beloved wife. From the moment we met, you presented yourself as royalty. Through your sacrifice, you have given me the opportunity to better serve our family and our generation. Thank you for praying Ruth Bell Graham's prayer–the same prayer she prayed for Billy Graham–for me when you were single. I love you with all my heart. I live for you and would gladly die for you a thousand times over.

To Hannah, the best girl in the whole world! Throughout history, wars have been fought over prized women. You are a young woman of such value. Never forget it! God has given you grace to unlock the hearts of kings, beginning with my own. I love you with all my heart.

To Jonathan, my son and my champion. I am extremely proud of you! I have never seen more exceptional character in a young man than in you. Even as your father, there are many qualities I admire in your life. Always be a man of impeccable character and integrity, even if you must courageously do so alone. I love you with all my heart.

To Alyse, my gracious God-daughter and amazing assistant. You are God's special gift to Sharon and me. You have the posture of a princess and the heart of a lioness. Thank you for being a fierce champion and defender of God's call on my life. I love you with all my heart.

To my precious mother, Sergeant Ammie Ward. My earliest memories in life are of you caring for me. I cannot begin to even grasp how much you've sacrificed for our family, but I'm profoundly grateful that you did. May God help me to ensure that your best days are ahead of you and not behind you. I am so incredibly proud of you Mom, and I love you immensely.

Don and Kandys, God's plan for you is great. I love you both and I'm grateful for your love. Be encouraged.

To Pastors Carlton and Sheila Arthurs. Dad, in my early twenties, you rescued me from ignorance and taught me to become wise. You taught me how to love Jesus, His Church, the Word of God, and Israel. God used you to make me who I am, by depositing your spiritual DNA into me. Mom, thank you for modeling what it means to be a gracious woman. To this day, your words of encouragement are most impactful. I love you both and will honor you all of my days.

To Dr. Robb and Pastor Linda Thompson. Dr. Robb, you have shown me that God's favor upon an individual's life is communicated through a person. He gave you keys to unlock my future and calling in life. Each time I enter your presence, I improve and learn to become more excellent in every way. Each conversation with you is memorable and enlarges my thinking. Thank you for embracing me as your own son. Pastor Linda, your smile, encouragement, and laughter strengthens me. I have never met a greater servant of Christ than you. I love you both and will honor you all of my days.

To Bishop Wellington and Katheryn Boone. Bishop, you were the first to inspire me to teach God's Word and challenge me to pursue big dreams. Each time I called you, you were there to help me "figure it out." I love you both and will honor you all of my days.

To the entire Ward, Arthurs, Nyong, and Krahenbuhl families. I could not have been placed into a better family context. I am inspired to be a better man each time we're together. I love each of you and am deeply grateful for your support.

To my publishing partners, Tom Freiling and Mike Klassen. I appreciate you more than I could ever express. Tom, our relationship is both divine and divinely appointed. I am honored to walk with you and have you as my coach in this arena. Thank you Jennifer Clark for your additional support.

To the James Ward Ministries Team and all my ministry partners, each of you believed in me, even before I fully understood my purpose and calling in life. You encouraged Sharon and me to believe that we could succeed. I especially want to thank Larry and Linda Layne, Bob, Demetress, and Reanetta Hunley, Darrell and Catherine Smith, Darryl and Christine Kilpatrick, Keith and Nicolette Jackson, and Natalie Everage Henderson for initially sharing the dream with us. David and Kathy Park, your ongoing encouragement rejuvenates us.

To the wonderful people of INSIGHT Church, Family Harvest Church, and Wheaton Christian Center, we are fortunate to have not one, but three church homes in the city of Chicago. Each time we come, we leave strengthened and encouraged. Thank you!

To all those who desire to end victim thinking and rise above the problems of this world, thank you for taking this journey with me, and for doing your part to make life better for those around you and the world a better place.

Preface

As tension continued to build, I squeezed my wife's hand before making my way toward the row of microphones. Cameras on and crowds of people pressing and jockeying for a better view, it seemed as if the whole world was watching.

Since third grade, God had been preparing and refining me for this exact moment. I sensed something was about to change and thought to myself, "I was born for this." God doesn't allow tragedy in which He does not triumph. By providence, God had chosen me and equipped me to share a message that He has spent a lifetime shaping for a time such as this–a message a hurting and divided nation desperately needed to hear. Emboldened by the words that the Holy Spirit had long ago engraved upon my heart, I spoke this message which was broadcast live on CNN and networks around the world:

Good afternoon everyone. My name is James E. Ward Jr., and along with my wife Pastor Sharon, we've been highly privileged to be the family pastor for more than thirty years to Miss Julia Jackson, the mother of Jacob Blake and also her mother, Janie Johnson...and at Julia's request and at attorney Crump's request, I want to just set the tone for our press conference today by briefly representing Julia's faith in the name of our Lord Jesus Christ and offer a brief word of prayer.

There are three types of law that govern a nation: spiritual law, moral law, and civil law, but we're only familiar with civil law, and we're often ignorant of the ramifications of violating spiritual and moral law which civil law alone cannot remedy. When these spiritual and moral foundations are destroyed, societies implode, people hurt each other. And what can the righteous do? So, we're calling our nation back to faith in God. Despite our differences, every citizen of America can agree that we indeed have a monumental problem in our nation, a problem that people created but people are incapable of solving. And, often, as we tell our church, we have a sin problem and not just a skin problem.

So, I invite you to join me in a brief moment of prayer as we ask our gracious God for His help during these very perilous times. Let's pray. Our father in Heaven, we humbly come to you in the name of our Lord Jesus Christ, and we ask you to forgive us all for straying from our ways, and from your ways, and from Your word, which invites the curse and results in repeated harming and the destruction of each other. I declare the mercy of God, the grace of God, the peace of God, the goodness of God, and most importantly the love of God over Kenosha, over black people and white people, over citizens and police, and over these United States of America. Father, unify us by Your Holy Spirit. We pray for Jacob Blake even now and ask you to heal his spirit, soul, mind, and body as well as the entire family. We ask You to give us wisdom on how to navigate our way forward as we deliberate to seek justice and to seek to bring healing to a hurting nation. In the name of our Lord Jesus Christ, we pray. Amen.

After I finished my words, I looked at my wife Sharon, and we both knew something was about to change in our lives and in our ministry. God was about to do a work through us that would impact the nation. Just a few days later, Sharon would answer a call from the President of the United States of America asking to speak with me. I had read Proverbs 22:29 many times. *Do you see a man who excels in his work? He will stand before kings; He will not stand before unknown men*. The Zero Victim message, which was birthed in my heart in third grade, was finally being released to America and even beyond.

As a black man raised in the deep south, I was surrounded by unspoken racial rules and tensions that twisted and tore people and communities apart. Witnessing the way the devil uses race to divide people, I have always instinctively known that we will be enslaved by victimhood if we let victim thinking take root. It insidiously winds its way around our hearts and minds, constricting like a serpent. Rejecting this way of thinking, even at a young age, I clung to the hope and healing that I found in Jesus Christ, and immersed myself in the message that He had placed within my heart.

This message, one of a Zero Victim Mentality, was a flame lit by the Lord and fanned into an incendiary conviction through His refinement in my life. The sharing of this message consumed me and became my ministry as I preached it over and over. Each time I did, something in me and in the people listening to me came alive. My resolve would be deepened and my mind renewed. As I faithfully taught and modeled Zero Victim thinking to my family and my church, sharing the lessons God laid on my heart, seeds were planted. And soon thereafter, I could see each of them shedding their victimhood thinking and blossoming into freedom.

Even as a man of faith, I could never foresee the events that were about to unfold. With our country in racial and political crisis, after months of COVID-19 quarantine, isolation and agitation spilled into our streets as people in turmoil attempted to punish others with their misery. Irrational voices clamoring to be heard drowned out reason and rational thought as people wreaked havoc in cities throughout our nation. Hurt people were hurting people and causing a storm of destruction and violence, clinging to victimhood to justify their actions in their unrighteous advance. Lives were destroyed, cities were razed, and yet the mob seemed unquenchable in its appetite for more destruction.

Justice was demanded, while authority was disregarded. People in pain were ravaging instead of reconciling. Lines were drawn, sides were chosen, and the devil reigned through manipulation, deception, and discord. Our nation was in peril as people picked political sides being more concerned about Right versus Left, than right versus wrong.

Just a few months after the death of George Floyd, amid this turmoil, Jacob Blake Jr. was shot seven times in the back in an incident involving Kenosha, Wisconsin police. Before facts were known, battle lines were formed, and riots began using his name to justify action on all sides. Jacob's mother, Julia Jackson, a dear woman of God and sister in Christ, and a member of my church, asked me to speak a word of calm at the family's press conference.

People experienced strong emotional reactions to this incident, forming irreconcilable opinions and lashing out on all sides. Politicians and opportunists hijacked this tragic event for their own gain. In each interview I was asked to give, the press pushed me to pick a side and to pit people against other people. Had I known beforehand, I would have done everything possible to avoid being where I was, yet I knew God had placed me there. In a society looking to both victimize and play the victim, it was time for me to deliver the only message capable of restoring rest in the streets of our nation.

With so much misery and agony in our nation, there still remains a need for change. Hurting people can only be truly healed by a transformation of the heart. In my address to the press, I spoke words reflecting the need for a change of heart. This sadness, violence, and desire for retribution we see in society is not new to our world. Society's problem is deeply rooted in sin, seeping out from deep with our very souls. Without a heart change, there will never be healing.

In the Bible, in the book of John, Jesus finds himself amid a mob of people intending to punish a woman guilty of committing adultery. We can imagine the push of the mob shouting and jostling, anger spilling over as they demand what they considered to be justice. Maybe the adulterous woman silently appealed to Jesus, crying for help, her eyes imploring Him for mercy. She had sinned, but didn't deserve death. The mob demanded the law, yet disregarded her humanity.

John 8:3-11 (NKJV) reads, *Then the scribes and Pharisees brought to Him a woman caught in adultery. And when they had set her in the midst, they said to Him, "Teacher, this woman was caught in adultery, in the very act. Now Moses, in the law, commanded us that such should be stoned. But what do You say?" This they said, testing Him, that they might have something of which to accuse Him. But Jesus stooped down and wrote on the ground with His finger, as though He did not hear. So when they continued asking Him, He raised Himself up and said to them, "He who is without sin among you, let him throw a stone at her first." And again He stooped down and wrote on the ground. Then those who heard it, being convicted by their conscience, went out one by one, beginning with the oldest even to the last. And Jesus was left alone, and the woman standing in the midst. When Jesus had raised Himself up and saw no one but the woman, He said to her, "Woman, where are those accusers of yours? Has no one condemned you?" She said, "No one, Lord." And Jesus said to her, "Neither do I condemn you; go and sin no more."*

The crowd is angry, and they are looking to Jesus to justify their anger. Because pain demands punishment, the mob looks to Jesus to agree that their idea of justice must be carried out. Then, Jesus does a very curious thing. He doesn't respond the way the mob expects him to. He bends down, quietly writing with His finger on the ground. At that moment, all eyes are drawn to Jesus. Instead of choosing sides or pointing fingers, He quietly draws their attention to himself. Only when their eyes are fixed on Him does He speak. Jesus asks them to examine their own hearts before seeking justice concerning the woman caught in sin.

Jesus never asked for a detailed list of her sins or required an explanation. He didn't demand a trial, but He did demand a change both from the accused and the accusers. God never chooses sides or plays to the political. He summons both sides to Himself. He calls the people to first look to Him and then to examine their own hearts. After fixing their eyes on Jesus and then examining their own hearts, the accusers realize the sin that lies within them. They recognize that the root of the problem is in their own hearts, and that they must judge themselves before casting stones of judgment at other people.

Still today, as emotions spill out onto our streets and riots continue to destroy, it is evident that there are problems in our nation that cannot be solved without radical change. All sides are demanding justice, but justice will never be found if a Biblical standard for what is right and true is not embraced. Victim thinking, emotional manipulation, political correctness, and cancel culture are the weapons used to intimidate and bully people into submission. This solves nothing. This heals nothing.

This changes nothing. Millions of people are blindly searching for answers while disregarding the answer that's already been given–Jesus.

My calling is to preach practical theology in contemporary culture, which is faith in Jesus applied to the social complexities of spirituality and intersectionality. Only when we turn our eyes to Him first, and then examine our own sinful hearts will we ever be able to move forward in a wave of change that engulfs our nation in the love of Christ, with liberty and justice for all. This is the answer. This is the only answer and final solution to injustice. Our hearts must be given to Jesus Christ for healing to take place, and our minds tempered with Zero Victim thinking.

This book is my letter of love and leading for you, sharing the victory over victimhood that I found in Christ. I first released Zero Victim in 2014, and the message is even more vital in today's divisive climate. In reading Zero Victim, it is my hope that your life will undergo lasting change, and that the lenses through which you see yourself and your life circumstances are transformed. I encourage you to look to Christ and then to examine your own heart. As our hearts change, the fabric of our nation will simultaneously be rewoven into a stronger fabric filled with faith and overflowing with love. It is my desire that each of us will be transformed by Christ to go and sin no more with a Zero Victim Mentality.

Introduction

Movements, movements, and more movements! I believe our society is suffering from a severe case of 'movements gone wild!' Presently, there are more than 115 major socio-political movements happening in America alone, not including the countless number of artistic, religious, and spiritual movements. In each case, individuals unite to fight for their beliefs, usually with limited perspective, to affect change around them, sometimes for better or sometimes for worse. But while people are quick to organize to affect change around them, in most cases, very little if any change is happening within them. How can unchanged people positively change the world around them? How can societies ever hope to be better if the people within them are not?

While movements can be powerful forces for good (or evil), could it be that the plethora of current socio-political movements are not indications of widespread cultural and systemic injustice, but a decline in personal character and erosion of individual morality? It seems as though individual identity and independent thinking have given way to identity politics, group think, and mob mentality. Each of us have felt the vice of mainstream ideologies attempting to squeeze us into ideological molds. It seems as if society presents us with a predefined, multiple choice test for every situation in life, and forces us to select A, B, C, or D. Essay answers are not permitted and asking questions will cause you to fail the exam. Don't think too much or too long. The exam is timed. Just pick your answer quickly from the choices you've been given.

To be fair, we must acknowledge that all social movements happen as a result of some truth. On many occasions movements begin as outcries of legitimate injustice or real need for change, but are quickly hijacked, perverted, hyper-inflated, politicized, weaponized, or transformed into something altogether different than what initially caused them to begin. The reaction of a newly formed movement often has little or nothing to do with the original action that made the movement necessary to begin with.

The Flaw With Movements

The flaw with movements is that they cannot ultimately effect change. Movements are only capable of bringing attention to situations that may legitimately need to be changed. If you burn your hand on a hot oven, a movement would be represented by your reactionary scream in pain, but screaming does not provide you with the intentional, strategic, and intelligent means to remove your hand, put on an oven mitt, or seek the appropriate medical attention. Many people involved in today's socio-political movements continue to scream in pain, but never move their hand away from the oven, after which their pain would automatically subside and their screams would be silenced. Screaming does not heal the injury. In some cases, I believe people get accustomed to screaming and actually learn to benefit from doing so. At a minimum, screaming gives them the attention they desire or need.

With respect, a current example of a movement that garners attention, but does not result in the change needed is the Colin Kaepernick movement. By kneeling during the pregame national anthem, Colin initiated a movement based upon his disapproval of the way black men were being treated by white police officers. This movement eventually spawned into a series of much more complicated issues that included politics, NFL policies and team owners, the American Flag, our military, Nike, Time magazine, and numerous other entities. But truthfully, what has Kaepernick's outspoken actions really changed? Did it actually solve the problem that caused him to protest? Have the number of incidents decreased? Is the relationship between white police officers and black men better? Has mutual respect and understanding been gained? How are things different now than before?

The challenge with many of these new movements is the fact that they are always relative and ambiguous. Today we have movements of anti-bullying, anti-capitalism, anti-facism (Antifa), anti-globalization, and anti-vaccination. Movements of feminism, ecofeminism, and free love. Organized movements such as Black Lives Matter, the Ku Klux Klan, LGBTQ, Men's Rights, Me Too, Occupy Wall Street, and Zeitgeist. Movements that are pro-choice, pro-life, veganism, and countless others.

These movements are becoming more polarized and more controversial. They appeal to some and offend others because their charters and founding premises are based upon subjective interpretations of moral law. But these various movements all have one thing in common. They all utilize the power of victim thinking, realizing that victimization–right or wrong–is a strong unifier, common denominator, and rally point among hurting people, and that victimization in some form is always the spark needed to ignite the conflagration of a new movement.

Movements Gone Wild!

Shamefully, many of today's movements are being compared to the various civil rights movements between 1919 and the 1960's in an attempt to validate them, but doing so is egregiously futile. Allow me to explain why.

Civil rights movements are intended to address violations of Constitutional Law and inalienable human rights. Such unlawful violations often discriminate against people based upon their ethnicity or natural gender, both unchangeable qualities of individual identity. Civil law violations sinfully contradict the fundamental value upon which our nation was built of liberty and justice for all. Through the efforts of courageous leaders, the unjust civil laws of the mid-1900's have been amended to provide equality for every legal citizen of the United States of America.

Most present-day socio-political movements do not address violations of Constitutional Law, but violations of relative, ever-shifting, individual preferences, and feelings associated with subjective interpretations of moral law. The fundamental flaw with this social construct is that every individual is permitted to define his/her own truth. We've sanctioned the notion that whatever I as an individual believe to be true for me is true. With more than 300 million citizens in our nation, that means there can be at least 300 million truths or opinions concerning issues we collectively face in society, because absolute truth no longer defines moral law.

Using the power of social media, any individual can broadly voice his/her own socio-political truth-opinion based upon their individual perspective. If enough misinformed people agree, a trend is started, a hashtag is created, and a new movement is born, capable of going viral and gaining global attention overnight. In an instant, victim thinking is mobilized globally.

"Most present-day socio-
political movements do
not address violations
of Constitutional Law,
but violations of relative,
ever-shifting, individual
preferences, and feelings
associated with subjective
interpretations of moral law."

What's Inside This Book?

Victim mentality is a perceived or conditioned mental tendency to regard yourself as a victim of the negative thoughts, words, or actions of others. It often provokes an individual to respond as if he/she really is a victim even when there is inadequate evidence. In this book, I will share practical steps on how you can identify, liberate, and protect yourself from victim thinking, by reconditioning and preconditioning your mind to rise above any act of injustice with a new attitude. You will not only learn how to reverse victim thinking, you will also be equipped and empowered to develop and maintain a Zero Victim Mentality through life's most difficult times and seasons.

The fact that you are even reading this book is proof that you see yourself winning in life and desire to do so. As you develop a Zero Victim Mentality, your days of fear, depression, discouragement, and offense will be eliminated altogether. The time has come for each of us as individuals, and collectively as a nation to rise above victimization with a bold, new attitude. We need a fresh start. Let's get started!

"Victim mentality is a perceived or conditioned mental tendency to regard yourself as a victim of the negative thoughts, words, or actions of others."

CHAPTER ONE

My Journey Toward a Zero Victim Mentality

My journey toward a Zero Victim Mentality began in 1983. I grew up in the southern United States, on the west side of Tuscaloosa, Alabama. Even in the early 1980s, race remained a significant issue in the South. Racial tensions simmered just below the surface and I intuitively knew the well-established unspoken racial rules.

Tuscaloosa's geography naturally encouraged the racial division of our city because the Black Warrior River literally divides the city in half. As a child, I understood that black people lived predominantly on the south side of the river and white people lived on the north side.

My family attended an all-black Baptist church and I attended an all-black elementary school. With the exception of my kindergarten and first grade teachers, I do not recall knowing any white people before third grade. But my experience after that changed my life forever.

School District Integration Opened My Eyes

After attending Central Elementary School kindergarten through second grade, the school board decided to integrate the school system. So in 1983, I transferred to a new school for third grade. Verner Elementary School was located on the north side of Tuscaloosa–the white side of town.

I vividly remember the bus ride to school on my first day. As we made our way from the south side to the north side of town, I couldn't help noticing a gradual improvement in the quality of living conditions. Less garbage lined the streets. The old Ford Thunderbirds and Chevy pickup trucks propped up on cinder blocks, were replaced by shiny new Dodge Caravans and Ford Country Squire station wagons.

Most noticeably, the homes were much nicer. Several mansions lined the road that led to our new school. Each day on my way to school I thought to myself, "Why can't I live in a home like that?" I didn't feel ungrateful for the loving home my parents provided for me, but something inside told me that I was good enough to live in one of those homes.

The first time I saw my new school, I was immediately impacted by the grandeur of it. The lawn was well manicured. The building was new and the playground was filled with working equipment! Nothing was broken down. Inside, sufficient lighting brightened the rooms, and the walls were painted with brilliant colors. The air smelled like fresh paint and new carpet. Every classroom contained new desks, a pencil sharpener that actually worked, and a brand new chalkboard. I instinctively knew that learning at this new school would be easier and much more enjoyable in comparison to my old school on the black side of town.

How My Third Grade Teacher Made a Difference in My Life

As I entered my classroom, my teacher, Mrs. Ruthie Pitts, greeted me. To my surprise, she was an African-American woman teaching on the white side of town. Still today, I remember Mrs. Pitts' appearance. Her professionally styled, salt-and-pepper hair never had one hair out of place. She was one of the most elegant women I'd ever seen. She sat at her desk with perfect posture, her hands clasped in front of her and her feet together. Her gracious appearance alone made an unforgettable impression on me.

Mrs. Pitts was different–she didn't talk or behave like most of the black people I'd known. I later learned that she lived on the black side of town, which seemed unusual. She was also a pastor's wife and a good friend of my grandmother.

Mrs. Pitts was articulate, professional, and extremely kind, but very tough. She encouraged me as a student, but seemed to hold me to a higher standard than my white peers. Although she never told me explicitly, I somehow understood she expected more from me.

I had heard many speeches before on the importance of doing well in school. Mrs. Pitts further explained to me the importance of getting involved in extracurricular activities to stimulate my social development. Huh? Unfortunately, all extracurricular activities occurred after school at the same time my bus departed for home. Mrs. Pitts was so committed to my involvement in these activities, she made arrangements with my parents and grandparents to bring me home from school each day.

I later discovered that Mrs. Pitts and I shared something in common. Although she was a teacher and I was a student, we were both embarking on an adventure of racial integration in the public school system. By attending my new school, I was taking advantage of the privilege and right so many African-Americans had previously fought for.

Racism and Discrimination Are Unnatural

I immediately made new friends at my new school, especially with the white kids. They seemed just as curious and eager to meet me as I was to meet them. I only have memories of genuine, caring relationships with my white childhood friends. I was often the only black kid involved in the after-school activities, and that's exactly what Mrs. Pitts wanted.

Fortunately, I cannot recall any racial slurs, experiences of marginalization, or feeling unfairly treated; only mutual respect, curiosity about diversity, and genuine interest in the opportunity to learn from someone with a different ethnic background. The relationships I formed with my white childhood friends taught me a valuable lesson–that racism and discrimination are unnatural. Something unfortunate happens in the lives of people that damages their thinking and causes them to develop such attitudes.

"The relationships I formed with my white childhood friends taught me a valuable lesson—that racism and discrimination are unnatural."

Day by day, my bus ride to school and my new friendships were changing my mentality. I became increasingly comfortable in my own skin and confident in my ability to relate to people who were different from me. The fear of being an "outsider" vanished. The more I got to know my white friends, the less I felt threatened by them. My appreciation for learning from their experiences, which were much different from mine grew. My new life among my new white friends on the white side of town, became a catalyst to help liberate me from victim thinking and the mentality of defeat.

A Zero Victim Mentality Is the Solution to Responding to Injustice

During my time in grade school, many teachers would write the names of misbehaving students on the chalkboard for everyone to see. On the other hand, Mrs. Pitts did so for academic excellence. I had always been a well-behaved, compliant, and straight-A student in grade school. As the year progressed, I noticed that my name often appeared on the chalkboard, and I was frequently identified as "student of the week."

One day the thought hit me like a bolt of lightning: *I am as smart as any other student in this classroom, boy or girl, black or white!* In an instant, my mentality changed forever. At eight years old, I realized that the color of my skin or growing up on the black side of town held no connection with my ability to succeed in school or in life. I understood that my success in life was not about comparing myself to others or competing with them, but about doing the very best that I could. I discovered that I ultimately controlled my own destiny and quality of life.

I began to observe some kids having fun at school and not doing their work, and getting bad grades as a result of their choices. As a black kid from the black side of town, with the help of Mrs. Pitts, I was able to mentally process what it meant to succeed among white students who were obviously more privileged than me, and had access to more resources than I did. In my mind, I did not penalize them for being privileged and living the way they lived. I wanted to live that way too.

I concluded that the white kids were not my enemy and could not hold me back. If I needed to work a little harder, I would. If anyone attempted to hinder me, I would not give in but would respond by increasing my efforts to succeed. As a result of my experiences in third grade, the Zero Victim Mentality seed was planted deep within my heart and mind, and still continues to grow to this day.

Unfortunately, systemic inequalities do still exist that often make life more difficult for non-whites in America, just as there are for women in a male-driven society. I'm saddened to admit that injustice is indeed an unchangeable fact of life for some people. I believe that developing a Zero Victim Mentality is the solution to responding to injustice in society. A Zero Victim Mentality empowers potential victims to rise above anger, insult, or unforgiveness toward those who initiated injustice against them, with a new attitude. This mindset prevents the recipient of the injustice from pointing the finger of blame toward others and changes their perception about it.

I'm Certified Zero Victim

Almost thirty years after sitting in Mrs. Pitts' third grade class, I was working as an assistant pastor in a large, racially diverse church in the south suburbs of Chicago. One day, the church's business manager informed the senior staff that we would all participate in a staff development exercise that required a personal assessment test.

Having completed several assessments in the past, I set low expectations for this new test. The business manager explained that this test was much different than the more common personality assessments. This attitude assessment test helps individuals understand how certain events, thoughts, beliefs, emotions, and perceptions impact them. Based upon his explanation, I took the assessment and waited for my results with anticipation.

Several weeks later, the assessment facilitator contacted me to review my test results. He began by explaining *catabolic energy*, a toxic energy that drains morale and can even destroy people and organizations. Catabolic energy results from thoughts and feelings of guilt, fear, worry, self-doubt, and low self-esteem. Catabolic energy typically creates an "I lose" frame of reference, which produces a tendency to hide and avoid people and issues, and causes people to live subject to their environment. People with high catabolic energy generally see themselves as victims in most situations and often suffer from depression and disengagement. In this first category that measured the degree to which I saw myself as a victim, my assessment result was zero percent.

With amazement, the facilitator commented to me, "In all of my years of facilitating this assessment, I've never seen anyone

"People with high catabolic energy generally see themselves as victims in most situations and often suffer from depression and disengagement."

score zero percent in the victim category! In your own words, I would like for you to explain this to me."

While attempting to explain my test results to the facilitator, I began to see how Zero Victim Mentality had been operating in, and guiding my life all along. Without knowing it, my Zero Victim Mentality ultimately defined all of my relationships and experiences in life, beginning with my encounter with Mrs. Pitts and my white friends in third grade.

CHAPTER TWO
Taking Personal Responsibility

Lewis had a troubled childhood. After his father abandoned them, Lewis and his mother endured a life of great difficulty. His mother worked two jobs while attending school part-time, leaving ten-year-old Lewis to fend for himself.

Without adult supervision, Lewis' questions about himself far exceeded his answers. Tormented by thoughts of rejection, he wandered most, "What did I do to cause my dad to leave our family? What's wrong with me? Why doesn't he love me?" Throughout his teen years and even as a young adult, Lewis blamed himself for the collapse of his family. Blame soon became guilt. This guilt would eventually result in low self-esteem, causing Lewis to lose confidence in his ability to succeed in anything. His grades were below average in school, all of his relationships seemed to repeatedly fail, and Lewis couldn't keep a steady job, often being terminated because of his anger issues.

Later in life, Lewis met Steve, a husband, a father of four, and a successful salesman. As their friendship grew, Lewis discovered Steve had a very similar childhood. "I know exactly what you're going through, Lewis. But take it from me, just because your childhood was troubled, doesn't mean that your future has to be! You must begin to see and think of yourself as a victor and not a victim, and things will soon change for the better!" Steve encouraged Lewis to simply make a present change in the way he saw his past, and to willfully change his attitude concerning his future.

Today, Lewis is also a husband and father of four. As Lewis' mentality and perspective changed, his circumstances, relationships, and career began to change proportionately. His life was no longer being defined and driven by the pain of his past, but by the purpose of his future. His thoughts of sadness were transformed into thoughts of success. Fear into faith. Hopelessness into hope. After thinking for years he must simply accept being born into disadvantaged circumstances, Lewis discovered a revolutionary principle. He discovered the secret to ending victim mentality and regaining control of the outcomes in his life, in every circumstance of life. Lewis learned how to become a Zero Victim thinker!

How would you like to immediately and permanently improve every area of your life? Imagine a life filled with more satisfying relationships with your friends, relatives, and co-workers. Picture being more effective and more productive in everything you do. Envision becoming a more influential leader who enables others to reach their maximum potential. Think what life would be like being free from the dark power of depression. You may be saying, "That's impossible! It sounds too good to be true!" However, I promise you something that is very much possible with God's help, and is also my present reality each and every day.

Let me be clear–this is not just another self-help book. I'm not at all opposed to them. I've owned plenty of them, many of which have benefited me greatly. While I appreciate the potential of self-help books to empower readers, my slight criticism is that they usually address only one specific area of need and are not holistic in their application. Self-help books are capable of making you strong in a particular discipline, while continuing to live an overall weak life.

What I will share with you in *Zero Victim* is a universal principle that can be applied to every area of your life. This principle will challenge you to intentionally and drastically change your perspective. It will cause you to see your present circumstances differently and allow you to realize new doors of possibilities standing right before you.

We All Want to Live Free!

Liberty is extremely important to us as American citizens. More than two hundred years ago, Thomas Jefferson drafted the Declaration of Independence and paved the way for the birth of the United States of America. In this important document, Jefferson explains that God our Creator granted all human beings certain "inalienable rights." Our government is commissioned to protect these rights, which are life, liberty, and the pursuit of happiness.

The words *life*, *liberty*, and *the pursuit of happiness* easily roll off the tongue. Yet, if we listed them in order of importance, they would appear as *liberty, the pursuit of happiness,* and *life. Liberty* would be placed first, because without liberty no one can pursue happiness. And consequently, life would not be worth living. Judging by his defiant words, it seems as if the lawyer, patriot, and former governor of Virginia, Patrick Henry, agreed when he brazenly proclaimed, "Give me liberty or give me death!"

When I speak in terms of *life*, I'm not referring to minimal existence on earth, characterized by misery and various forms of physical and mental oppression. Who wants to live a long life when life is hell on earth? On the contrary, I consider *life* to mean maximal existence on earth, characterized by extraordinary happiness and complete personal freedom. In this book, we'll see that happiness and freedom begin in our minds.

Life also includes mental freedom, and mental freedom means freedom from the mentality of defeat and the life altering effects of injustice. In order to overcome injustice, we must first adopt the same attitude as Patrick Henry by boldly announcing, "Give me mental liberty or give me death!" Mental liberty is Zero Victim thinking, which empowers you to intentionally change your way of looking at the world. Why is mental liberty so critical? Because more than anything else, it determines the extent to which we can be happy and free regardless of the conditions and people surrounding us. Our mentality or mode of thought ultimately determines the quality of our lives.

Put on Your Oxygen Mask First!

I was highly motivated to write this book because I passionately desire for you to live a life that is holistically wealthy. I'm not only referring to material wealth, I'm also referring to the immaterial wealth of healthy self-esteem, peace of mind,

"Mental liberty is Zero Victim thinking, which empowers you to intentionally change your way of looking at the world."

happiness, quality relationships, and many other riches, which I believe are more valuable than money.

Nothing pains me more than seeing people with unlimited potential held back by the limitation of victim thinking. As victim thinking is removed, you will experience greater motivation in life and more clearly see that there are no limits to what you can achieve. The odds can be beaten. Disabilities and inabilities can be overcome. The fallen can arise. The broken can be restored. These are all possible when each person refuses to accept that they are victims, and terminates enslavement by victim thinking with Zero Victim Mentality.

While reading this book, I give you permission to be unashamedly selfish by focusing exclusively on the development of your own mindset. Throughout my years as a husband, father, and leader in various organizations, I have discovered that unselfishness begins with a certain degree of selfishness. Think about it. We cannot take others where we have not been, or model for them what we have not experienced. I want you to experience total freedom from victim thinking, which will empower you to impact those around you in greater ways.

Before a commercial airplane takes off, the flight attendant stresses the importance of every passenger securing their own oxygen mask before assisting the people around them. In order to liberate others in life, we must begin by liberating ourselves and also maintaining our liberty.

The struggle for mental liberty is often the fight of our lives. It will not come easily. Negative thoughts and experiences, including fear, insecurity, injustice, and guilt, turn our minds into battlefields. Here we must engage, outmaneuver, and ultimately

"As victim thinking is removed, you will experience greater motivation in life and more clearly see that there are no limits to what you can achieve."

defeat negative thoughts. Our mind is the place where victories in life are initially won. If you can learn to consistently win victories in your minds, victories in and over your circumstances will soon follow.

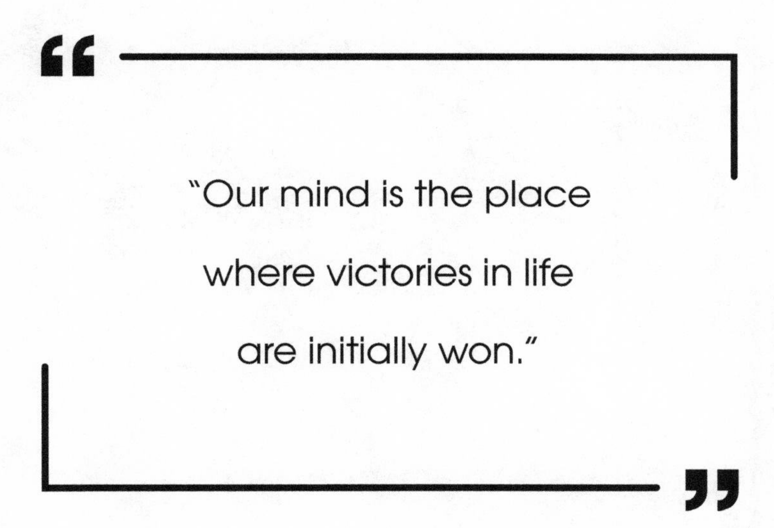
"Our mind is the place
where victories in life
are initially won."

CHAPTER THREE
The World Is a Hostile Place

Judging by the many unfortunate events we see and hear about each day, we could certainly describe the world to be a rather hostile place. By hostile I mean that life at times can be seemingly antagonistic, in which circumstances are working against us. Some kind of counter force is necessary on our behalf to bring balance, if we will avoid becoming victims of these circumstances in life.

Without specific actions of strategic intervention such as education, employment, and exercise, our lives would quickly become dysfunctional. Like teeth and rocks that naturally decay, our lives will do the same without some form of intervention. Those who fail to seek help when necessary may even die an early death. The Centers for Disease Control (CDC) recently reported that approximately 900,000 Americans die prematurely, yet up to 40 percent of those deaths could be prevented. Life naturally intends to make victims out of each of us. Therefore, we must intentionally and strategically work against the circumstances that work against us.

All relationships need specific care and intervention to prevent them from decaying. None of us can survive alone. Perhaps more than we are willing to admit, we desperately need each other to survive and thrive. We especially need relationships with our family members, but even in the context of our immediate families, hostilities exist.

One Man's Journey in a Hostile World

I want to share with you a story of an exceptional young man. Born into a large family, he (along with his brothers) supported their father in managing their large family estate. The eleventh of twelve sons, this young man experienced the cruelties and criticisms commonly associated with victimizations experienced by younger siblings. As a teen, he only desired to be faithful to his father and diligently fulfill his duties on the family estate.

This young man was gifted intellectually and skilled administratively. At an early age, he demonstrated extraordinary vision. He quickly became his father's favorite child among his brothers, who consistently proved to be recklessly irresponsible and untrustworthy.

Motivated by his deep love for his favorite son, the father did special things for this young man publicly without considering the sentiments of his brothers, or the impact it would have on their relationship with their younger brother.

Whenever the father was absent, the younger brother suffered constant taunting and name-calling by the older brothers. Fueled

"Life naturally intends
to make victims out
of each of us."

by jealousy, they seized every opportunity to put the younger brother "in his place" by reminding him of his inferior status within the family. In every situation, the younger brother felt hated, excluded, disrespected, and rejected.

The younger brother's life became characterized by undeserved persecution and injustice from his own family. Oppression from the hand of an enemy is more understandable than oppression from a family member. The emotional agony of being intentionally injured by a loved one–someone you expect to lovingly care for you–someone with whom you should feel safe–can be unbearable. We expect to be celebrated and not victimized by our family members.

The young man's ability to dream became his only escape from his nightmare of harassment, injustice, and victimization. One night, the younger brother dreamed he ruled over his entire family, and they bowed before him. Unfortunately, he shared his dream with the very people who were responsible for creating his living nightmare. Because of his dream, his father scolded him and his brothers hated him even more.

As a teen, the younger brother's troubles were just beginning. As his brothers were tending their father's flocks in a distant land, the father decided to send his favorite son to assess their well-being, as they were too irresponsible to report home. The older brothers' deep hatred toward their younger brother began to stir as they observed his approach. They plotted to kill him. Just before doing so, they decided to throw him into a pit and later sold him as a slave to foreign merchants who took him far away from his home country. The brothers were relieved to know that their younger brother's dream of ruling over them would never become a reality.

Considered Guilty until Proven Innocent

After being taken away from home, the younger brother was sold again to another slave owner. His new master, a nobleman, had an immoral wife who attempted to seduce the young man. Angered by his refusal, the nobleman's wife falsely accused him of attempted rape. He was wrongly convicted of a crime without a trial, and sentenced to prison.

It seemed that his life was only filled with painful memories of victimization and injustice, even though he had always maintained his integrity. The young man was undeservingly hated by his brothers, reprimanded by his father, thrown into a pit, twice sold into slavery, falsely accused, convicted, and sentenced to prison. But by maintaining a Zero Victim Mentality, he never permitted the storyline of his unfortunate past to write the script of his future. For his entire life, the younger brother had lived as a victim of extreme injustice. Yet, despite the opposition he endured, the younger brother's dream eventually came true.

If you haven't guessed by now, I have been recounting the Biblical story of Joseph, the son of Jacob. His story is one of the greatest examples of how good people can and should respond when bad things happen to them at no fault of their own.

Bad Things Do Happen to Good People

Each day, news commentators report calamities happening around the world to hundreds and thousands of innocent people. Thousands more go unnoticed and unreported. Daily news reports seem like nothing more than a recap of every injustice that occurred throughout the day–a roll call of the latest victims of murder, theft, school and workplace shootings, sexual misconduct, white-collar crimes, and terrorist attacks. These tragedies have become synonymous with our existence. We no longer respond in shock when we hear of them. We're slowly becoming desensitized to injustice and the victimization of innocent people. Victimization has become an expected way of life.

Sometimes these calamities are accidental. Sometimes we see examples of events that can only be described as evil being intentionally perpetrated by people toward other people. Who can forget the gruesome day on September 11, 2001, when America witnessed the loss of 2,977 innocent lives because nineteen terrorists hijacked four airplanes, crashing two of them into the World Trade Center towers? Innumerable tragedies occur every day around the world, turning innocent people into victims.

Something Is Terribly Wrong

Considering the magnitude and frequency of tragic reports we hear about every day, we must conclude that something is terribly wrong with the world. Imperfect people create and manage an imperfect world around them. Therefore, victimization and injustice are inevitable. You could say life's default design produces victims, regardless of age, ethnicity, social status, or gender. Victimization is a common denominator that unites all individuals throughout the world. It connects black men with Jewish women; Jewish women with Hispanic men; Hispanic men with Asian women. Victimization is timeless, universal, and nondiscriminatory. Being born fulfills the only qualification necessary to experience injustice in this life.

“Being born fulfills the only qualification necessary to experience injustice in this life.”

I believe people in the world should be more united by a common need and desire to avoid victimization, instead of divided by our religious, socio-economic, political, racial, or gender differences. We all deal with some form of past or present pain. Furthermore, we're all destined to encounter future circumstances that will potentially present us with many more, and greater pitfalls of victimization.

I don't intend to be ominous, but victimization is simply a part of life in a hostile world. Therefore, we are wise to anticipate occasions where we might be victimized, and preempt those occasions by developing Zero Victim thinking. While doing so, we must not live in fear, but should prepare ourselves to prudently deal with victimization appropriately when it comes.

There Are So Many Everyday Victims

Now that we've identified the hostile nature of the world, let's explore how circumstances attempt to bring about victimization on a personal level. The hostilities I refer to are not "out there." They begin within your mind and are only triggered by external circumstances. Each of us face a unique set of challenges and pitfalls, constantly attempting to make victims out of us. This attack relentlessly continues each moment of every day. No two people face the same set of challenges in life, but we all have them. Let's take a closer look at the lives of several people–everyday people like you and me, who must fight mental battles of victimization.

"We are wise to anticipate
occasions where we
might be victimized,
and preempt those
occasions by developing
Zero Victim thinking."

Olivia

Olivia struggles as an unmarried woman and single-mother of one child. As far back as she could remember, she dreamed of the perfect day she would stand before the altar, dressed in her mother's wedding gown, to marry the man of her dreams. Olivia's greatest desire was to be a loving wife and caring mother. While working toward her bachelor's degree in accounting, she met Brad during her junior year in college.

Olivia and Brad began to date and soon fell in love, or so she thought. On several occasions, she cautiously disclosed her deep desire to marry, but noticed how Brad became uncomfortable and slightly irritated during those discussions. As the two of them spent more time together, Olivia became even more fond of Brad and found herself helplessly attached to him emotionally. She concluded that he was her soul mate and the man she wanted to spend the rest of her life with.

After several days of unusual illness, Olivia's best friend encouraged her to take a pregnancy test. To Olivia's disbelief, she discovered she was pregnant and immediately called Brad. Just a few weeks later, Brad transferred to a different college out of state, and Olivia dropped out of school altogether. Six years later, she would often find herself awake at night, alone, crying, and thinking, "How could he do this to me?" Olivia concluded she could never again trust a man. Unfortunately, she and her child suffered injustice as a result of Brad's selfish desires and immaturity.

Fred

For forty-one years, Fred worked for Diamond Textiles, Inc. Known for his decades of faithfulness, Fred inspired the workers around him. He survived the dynasties of four CEOs and endured three major economic downturns. Fred and his wife decided he would retire at age sixty-five, at which time they would travel. Most of all, they were looking forward to spending more time with their grandkids.

During a routine staff meeting, Fred and his coworkers received devastating news. Several company executives were charged with using accounting loopholes and false financial reporting to cover millions of dollars of debt from failed business transactions.

The company's CFO was indicted for intentionally misleading Diamond Textiles' board of directors. Having filed for Chapter 11 bankruptcy, the company lost millions of dollars in pensions. Fred asked the HR Director in dismay, "So what about my retirement?" The Director replied, "I'm sorry, Fred. There's just nothing there." Having faithfully worked at Diamond for over four decades, Fred suffered injustice and became a victim of corporate fraud and lost the majority of his retirement savings.

Lisa

With the tenacity, focus, and shrewdness of a multimillion-dollar real estate broker, 13-year-old Lisa was the most successful seller of Girl Scout cookies in the Midwest region. Her bedroom had become a trophy room, filled with numerous awards she received for exceptional performance in cookie sales. Years later, Lisa completed her undergraduate studies in Business Administration Summa Cum Laude, and later earned an MBA with honors from a prestigious university.

After a successful internship with a Fortune 500 company, Lisa accepted a full-time position on their platinum sales team. Within months, she broke new records by shattering historical benchmarks with her third quarter sales performance.

While celebrating their success at a team dinner, Lisa's coworker Bobby, casually mentioned his excitement for receiving his first big bonus check in the amount of $25,000. At that moment, Lisa realized her male coworker received a much larger bonus than she did, despite his marginal performance with fewer qualifications. For the first time in her new career, Lisa experienced injustice and became a victim of gender discrimination in corporate America.

Juan

Being the first person in his family to attend college, Juan was an exceptional student and leader among his peers. He earned his place in multiple academic honor societies and several other prestigious organizations. Raised in Mexico, Juan excelled as a soccer player and served as the captain of the university's championship soccer team.

In college, Juan developed close friendships with William and Ted, both members of the elite Chi Omega Tau fraternity. For two years, William and Ted encouraged Juan to join their fraternity. Because of his academic, social, and athletic success, they felt that he would be a great addition to their fraternity. Juan reluctantly decided to apply in order to establish a closer bond with his friends.

Several weeks later, Juan received a letter from the president of the fraternity informing him his application to join was denied. Disappointed, Juan informed William and Ted, who scheduled

“Repeated victimization tends to destroy an individual’s positive outlook by permanently creating negative memories and damaged emotions.”

a private meeting with their fraternity brothers to understand why. After several hours of probing for an explanation of why Juan would not be allowed to join the fraternity, the membership council of the fraternity unanimously stated that Juan simply wasn't a "good fit" for Chi Omega Tau. Juan suffered injustice and became a victim of racial discrimination in his attempt to establish a closer bond with his friends.

They Keep Asking, "Why Me?"

Olivia, Fred, Lisa, and Juan all suffered injustice having experienced the victimization of simply living in a hostile world. They were all only guilty of being themselves. You may relate. Regardless of our best efforts to do things right and do the right thing, every one of us has been a victim of some form of injustice. We all endure difficulties at no fault of our own. Let's face it–we live in a world where imperfect people develop imperfect systems, that frequently victimize the people who operate within those systems. Victimization not only happens on an individual level, but also systemically on an institutional level.

At some point in our lives, we all wonder, *Why me?* Behind that question lies innocence battered by some form of undeserved injustice. Repeated victimization tends to destroy an individual's positive outlook by permanently creating negative memories and damaged emotions. Negative past experiences impact us greatly by conditioning our mentalities and shaping our perspectives. Our only solution to this dilemma is to protect ourselves against the hostilities of life by developing a programmed mindset to overcome injustice and recognize victory in every situation.

CHAPTER FOUR
Ideological and Emotional Warfare

It is estimated that as many as 85 million fatalities occurred in WWII. By far, it was the bloodiest war in human history. I solemnly honor the ultimate sacrifice of every life given and mourn the loss of every life taken, but I believe our world is heavily engaged in a new kind of conflict that has produced even more fatalities. I describe this new conflict as ideological and emotional warfare.

In addition to many casualties of war, this intangible conflict also produces an innumerable number of emotional POWs and hostages, and countless more that are maimed and carry battle scars. The gruesome analogy of war helps us better understand just how barbaric victim mentality can be. On several recent occasions, we've seen how perceived injustice is capable of producing extremely violent, vitriolic, and irrational reactions by those offended, which in some cases even result in the loss of lives.

Judging from these violent reactions to offense, it seems that victim thinking in the minds of these offended individuals is so deep, they respond as if they sincerely believe their life is in danger. Once an individual believes that their life is in danger, the use of violence or even deadly force in self-defense becomes justified. Although a tangible weapon is not present and no physical assault has occurred, a deeply offended victim thinker is afraid of being murdered emotionally, which can feel just as real as if someone is attempting to take their life physically. Ideological and emotional warfare can quickly and easily turn violent because the mind itself is the battlefield.

We Need A New Attitude!

I believe the initial key in creating the right frame of mind to overcome injustice, offense, emotional wounds, and victim thinking is the willful and intentional, strategic development of a new attitude. I want to remind you that attitude is a choice! The inner plights of victimization don't go away easily or just fade away over time. Intentional intervention is needed to foster healing of the heart and mind. You may have heard the phrase, "Time heals all wounds." But I don't believe that to be true at all. On the contrary, time makes unresolved pain worse as we spend days, hours, and years rehearsing and meditating on unpleasant and unfortunate memories.

Attitude can be generally defined as a decisive, mental point of view about someone or something. I describe attitude as both a mental position and a mental disposition. Your mental position is what you presently believe. Your mental disposition is what you have a tendency to believe in the future, which can also be described as your outlook. Whatever attitude you presently hold,

"Intentional intervention is needed to foster healing of the heart and mind."

shaped by your past, will be reflected in your future behavior. I've discovered that inappropriate behavior can be corrected by replacing and preempting wrong emotions with right attitudes.

When right attitudes have been decided upon, emotions follow instead of leading. As I observe American culture and various interactions on social media platforms, I see a generation of people being led by their feelings and emotions instead of decisive attitudes of choice. I believe many people like me, are greatly frustrated and tired of all the negativity we see reflected in people's words and behavior. I believe the American people and people of other nations are ready for, and desperately in need of a new attitude concerning our response to injustice and offense.

Rebellion Against the Status Quo

This shift from negativity to positivity will not come by conforming to the state of our culture as it is. A mental rebellion against the status quo is needed! No matter what cable news channel you watch or what publication you read, each of them report on socio-political ills from their own limited and biased perspective. This approach creates polarized "camps" which allow people to hunker down and become more deeply and immovably entrenched in their side's position. As a result, division between both sides continues to increase and cannot be bridged.

Real and acceptable solutions are rarely offered to eliminate the socio-political problems we face. And when they are, the other side remains staunchly opposed to whatever recommendations are made, simply because the recommendations originated on the other side. In each instance, a stalemate is reached. I sincerely believe Zero Victim Mentality is the new perspective and new

“When right attitudes
have been decided upon,
emotions follow instead
of leading.”

attitude our society desperately needs and is longing for. This new way of thinking calls both opponents out of their corners to the center of the boxing ring. If we intend to move forward in developing and maintaining a peaceful and harmonious society, a change in attitude is needed.

We cannot address new problems and never-seen-before challenges with old attitudes and outdated perspectives. I believe this is one of the reasons why we're seeing so little progress toward unity, reconciliation, and healing. New problems and new challenges in society must be met with new attitudes and new positive perspectives if forward progress will be made. This new attitude must include respecting those with beliefs and values different than our own, without demonizing them or slandering their character because they hold different beliefs.

Past Progress

By studying history, we can see how past generations embraced and overcame what seemed to be insurmountable social challenges at the time. Unfortunately, since the time humans first began to occupy earth, injustices have occurred and lives have been lost. But each time, somehow, some way, the people overcame, and a pivotal moment in history occurred that launched humanity into a new era of growth, development, innovation, and opportunity. Even while still under their present challenge, in each case, a historical shift began with a group of fearless individuals who were futuristically positive in their perspective, and did not accept that they were victims in the moment.

"The level of difficulty in dealing with social challenges is not getting higher. Personal emotional thresholds are getting lower."

It seems that each successive generation in today's society is progressively moving away from sound reasoning toward hyper-emotionalism. It seems that younger people are much more delicate emotionally, and not nearly as tough as children in previous generations. I recall my father telling stories of the life he and his siblings lived as children. To say the least, their lives were hard. Very hard! Certainly more difficult than the life of the average child today. But in a good way, their tough life produced tough children. Children who grew up finding intelligent solutions to their problems, instead of wallowing in the pitiful emotions of their victimization.

Just maybe, each generation is becoming more sensitive and more soft. I believe that this is why the impact of the same social challenges people have faced for decades is intensifying, and social problems are becoming more difficult to solve. More than ever before, people are processing those same challenges emotionally instead of intelligently. The level of difficulty in dealing with social challenges is not getting higher. Personal emotional thresholds are getting lower.

Ironically, colleges and universities designed to teach our students to reason and think critically, are creating "safe zones" for students to process their challenges emotionally instead of intellectually. As a result, college campuses are mass producing many POWs, hostages, and casualties of ideological and emotional warfare. More and more college students are being marginalized because their convictions and beliefs are not aligned with those more generally accepted by mainstream society.

"The level of difficulty in dealing with social challenges is not getting higher. Personal emotional thresholds are getting lower."

EWMDs: Emotional Weapons of Mass Destruction

The concept of *weapons of mass destruction* was first used in response to the development of chemical, biological, and nuclear weapons. The phrase reverberated across America and subsequently the world during the time when President George W. Bush sought to dismantle the regime of the Iraqi President and dictator, Saddam Hussein. The grave concern of a terrorist possessing weapons of mass destruction is the immediate, widespread annihilation of millions of people before a threat can even be identified.

Today's society has a growing number of new terrorists at-large who are actively destroying millions of people by using emotional weapons of mass destruction. Enabled and empowered by the various and pervasive platforms of broadcast and social media, these emotional terrorists are now targeting entire people groups with the intent of destroying them, by weaponizing their emotional vulnerability.

People groups that have historically and unfortunately dealt with legitimate acts of injustice are being manipulated and indoctrinated to believe that there is a literal war on women, gays, Blacks, Whites, Hispanics, Muslims, and many other people groups. Everyone is at war with everyone! Knowing that past injustices stir the emotions of those affected by them, emotional terrorists and purveyors of victim thinking have learned a powerful truth. They have learned to control and mislead those people groups by reminding them of their pain and manipulating their emotions. I am saddened to say that some, but certainly not all politicians, social justice advocates, and even pastors, have learned the art of skillfully using this new form of ideological and emotional warfare.

Emotional Hackers

In some cases, computer hackers have no desire to destroy operating systems. It is much more profitable, purposeful, and gratifying for them to gain control of a perfectly good operating system to be used at their malevolent discretion. Emotional hackers have learned how to leverage digital media and social media platforms to hack into people's emotions, win their allegiance, and gain significant control of their lives and even financial resources for their own socio-political use.

The hackers have discovered that emotions are much more powerful than intellect. They are not trying to intelligently persuade people to join their cause. More effectively, their aim is to get people to feel their cause and to emotionally sway people, knowing that their core beliefs, decisions, and financial resources will soon follow their emotions.

Many women continue to fall in love with, and follow men they know are not good for them because their emotions have been hacked. Millions of men irrationally gamble away the family's mortgage and grocery money, or yield to a seductress because their emotions have been hacked. Perfectly good relationships are often damaged and destroyed, not by mental decisions made, but by emotional sentiments felt.

More than any other period in the history of our nation, voters are voting according to what they emotionally feel about candidates and political issues, in place of what they know to be factually true about those candidates and their proposed policies.

This phenomenon explains why tension is growing surrounding the same challenges our nation has been facing for centuries. We are becoming more and more divided, citing irreconcilable differences over issues that people in past generations have been able to cordially and intelligently resolve. All of this is happening because people are feeling more than they are thinking.

Instead of sitting down to collaborate and develop comprehensive solutions to our southern border crisis, politicians would rather tell stories of how many families are being separated and how many children are suffering. Well of course they're suffering...It's a border crisis! But don't just pander about it. Fix it! The border crisis or any other crisis will not be resolved by appealing to people's emotions to make them feel bad about the crisis, or to demonize those they believe are responsible for it.

Crisis can only be resolved when intelligent thought is utilized to do so. If we're intelligent enough to send people to the moon, we're intelligent enough to solve our border issue. So what's the delay? I believe political pundits and emotional hackers have discovered that the southern border crisis is valuable socio-political-emotional capital, easily used to move people at the polls.

Falling From Facts to Feelings

I believe our nation is on a moral decline, partly because society continues to fall from objective reasoning to subjective emotionalism–from facts to feelings. Even our institutions of higher education are being affected and increasingly defined by this. What we previously considered to be bastions of critical thought and objective reasoning, have in some cases become brothels of emotional manipulation and subjective syllogism.

"What we previously
considered to be bastions
of critical thought and
objective reasoning, have in
some cases become brothels
of emotional manipulation
and subjective syllogism."

It seems that every controversial issue in today's society has been hijacked by feelings and emotions. Debates about abortion, gay marriage, gender identity, use of the Conferedate flag, the statues of Confederate war heroes, first amendment rights, racism, heathcare, and many others have all become issues that are deeply emotional, and are usually engaged emotionally more so than logically. We have to wonder why people are suddenly and so deeply bothered by issues that have existed in society for many years. I believe it is because we are increasingly becoming a nation of victim thinkers.

Living by feelings presents a great liability in life. It is nearly impossible to win a game if the field is constantly shifting and the rules are ever-changing. A popular Bible verse asks the question, "If the foundations are destroyed, what can the righteous do?" (Psalm 11:3). Traditional moorings and Biblical foundations of truth in our society are being questioned, contested, and destroyed, which undermines the advancement of communal practices that are truly righteous.

Because of the extreme emotional volatility we're seeing in response to social issues, our world is becoming more unstable. Social stability can only be established in societies where people righteously and morally live from the inside-out, and not from the outside-in. A person who lives life from the outside-in will become society's yo-yo. Having little or no control over external circumstances, our first step in overcoming the challenges we face is to first overcome those challenges within.

Time to Act!

It is simply impossible to ever dig yourself out of a pit of victimization, if the purveyors of victim thinking keep dumping emotional dirt on your head. As a Christian, black American man, this is my personal challenge with the way black Americans are often related to. It seems as though the intelligent prospect of forward advancement is overshadowed by the emotional pain of our journey to get where we presently are (Which by the way is a fantastic place, comparatively speaking from a global perspective.).

Of course there are important lessons to be learned from the past, but rehearsing the pain of the past will never help us step into the purpose of our glorious future. We all have limited time to act and change to move forward. The most precious resource on earth is not tangible, but intangible. It's time. It's the precious grains of sand that keep falling through the hourglass of life. You must act in time, realizing it's time to act, before it's too late.

This book has been written to serve as a spiritual, mental, and moral guide to help you recalibrate your emotional compass. It will also serve as a powerful offensive and defensive weapon in your arsenal, as you engage in the deadly conflict of ideological and emotional warfare. This book will enable you to adequately protect and defend yourself and your family against the many emotional weapons of mass destruction formed against you. With a Zero Victim Mentality, none of them will prosper!

Without a moral map to help you navigate through the rough terrain and treacherous waters of victim thinking and hyper-emotionalism which define our society, your journey may be fatal. I encourage you and challenge you to *zero out* and reset your emotions by fully embracing and adopting a Zero Victim Mindset.

CHAPTER FIVE

My Identity as a Christian, Black American Man

I am unapologetically and unashamedly a follower of Jesus Christ. Even if my life was at stake, I simply cannot deny the reality of my personal, transformative experience with God through faith in Christ. To deny the depth of my conviction would be to deny my very person. The same conviction I have to live for Christ reminds me that other people are under no obligation to believe what I believe (although I wish they would because of the temporal and eternal benefits of doing so).

The essence of Biblical Christianity is something Jesus describes as being *born again*. Every human is accustomed to celebrating the day of his/her birth each year. That day is considered special because it reminds us of the day we were naturally born into this world. When speaking with Jesus about the *born again* experience, a Jewish leader asked Jesus, "How can a man enter a second time into his mother's womb?"

In response, Jesus began to explain what it means to be *born again*. The first birth is experienced by every human on earth, but the second birth is a spiritual birth. Jesus explained to the Jewish man that it is possible to be alive naturally, but dead spiritually. That humans only "come alive" and live spiritually when they are *born again* through faith in Jesus Christ as Savior and Lord. I will explain more about the significant role faith in Christ plays in the development of a Zero Victim Mindset in the Appendix section of this book.

The point of me describing the Christian *born again* experience is to share how indispensable it is in defining my identity and character. Whether Christian or non-Christian, every human derives their identity and character from some source. That source may be connected to their family, faith, culture, ethnicity, or gender. For me and many other *born again* Christians like me, our identity and character are primarily based upon God's Word. As Christ-followers, the Bible informs us (or should) what to say, how to think, how to feel, how to conduct ourselves in this life, and even how to process unfortunate circumstances in life–that we should represent Christ on earth in every way.

I was naturally born as a black American male, as the son of James and Ammie Ward. But I was spiritually *born again* as a son of God through faith in Jesus Christ. As much as I love and cherish my biological parents, and appreciate the life they gave me and the wonderful legacy I was born into, my spiritual rebirth through faith in Christ is infinitely more important and more significant to me that my natural birth. Before coming to faith in Christ, my

"The victimization of racism simply doesn't work on me because I'm secure in my identity in Christ."

life was defined by my birth, but has since been redefined by my rebirth.

I Love My Enemies!

You may be wondering why and how being *born again* is relevant in my development of a Zero Victim Mentality. The answer is because the *born again* experience provided me with a new identity that is far superior to my ethnicity, skin color, height, weight, gender, or socio-economic status. My identity in Christ elevates me above all of the common issues in life that are used and even weaponized to cause people to become victims.

I am in no way advocating for us to remain passive in redressing all types of injustice, nor am I suggesting we turn a blind eye to them. Doing so would be sinful. Although I am deeply desirous of racial equality in a world of racial inequality, I am not, nor can I be victimized by racism because my identity in Christ has been secured. The victimization of racism simply doesn't work on me because I'm secure in my identity in Christ. Knowing who I am in Christ has empowered me to be unaffected by any would be racist, and even sincerely love them as does Christ.

As a Christ-follower, Jesus has commanded and supernaturally empowered me to love my enemies. I am often disappointed to see others who claim to be Christian respond to injustice in ways that are void of faith and grossly inconsistent with the teachings of Christ. Every Christian must be Christian first!

Heaven will not be populated with only black people, white people, Hispanics, Indians, Asians, Native Americans, etc. It will not be a segregated place. Heaven will be populated with one new

"My identity in Christ elevates
me above all of the common
issues in life that are
used and even weaponized
to cause people to
become victims."

race of people–the righteous redeemed–those who have been *born again* as children of God, and just happen to have slightly different amounts of melanin in their skin. When Jesus tells us to pray *on earth as it is in Heaven*, perhaps He was telling us that racial reconciliation originates in Heaven in the presence of God our Creator, and simply isn't possible without His help.

Despite his misguided values and corrupt way of thinking, the Imperial Wizard of the Ku Klux Klan is loved by Christ, and loved by me. Let's be clear. I am not at all suggesting that Christ nor I approve of his actions. But I am referring to a willful decision to love him, empowered by God's love for all, and God's desire to redeem their lives. Jesus died to save every misguided member of the KKK.

This standard of love is not possible for James the black American son of James and Ammie Ward to uphold, but is very possible for James the son of God to uphold, empowered by God's own love. My identity in Christ has empowered me to rise above any offense associated with racism and racial injustice with a new attitude.

Black American, Not African American

Whenever I'm specifically asked, I refer to myself as black American and not African American. Generally speaking, Blacks in America are typically all of African descent. With the exception of those who may have traced their heritage through modern DNA testing, most Blacks in America have no idea what specific country or people group in Africa their ancestors were part of.

"The term *African-American*
is vague and contributes
to what I believe to be a
looming issue of identity crisis
among black Americans."

On multiple occasions, I have visited several countries on the beautiful continent of Africa. But when I'm there, I am as much a foreigner in those African countries as I would be in China, Brazil, or Norway, even though my skin color and facial features are quite similar to the people around me. The darker color of my skin, similar facial features, and my African ancestry are irrelevant in making me feel at home or less like a foreigner in any African country I visit. I have no direct connection to the culture or the people. I have never visited Africa and thought to myself, "It's sure is good to be home!" I dress like an American. I eat like an American. I talk like an American. I think like an American. Why? Because I'm black American, not African American.

The term *African-American* is vague and contributes to what I believe to be a looming issue of identity crisis among black Americans. There are fifty-four distinct nations on the continent of Africa. To vaguely say that I am African-American still means that there are fifty-four possible unique cultures and ethnicities for me to be associated with. As an African American, I am faced with many more identity challenges to sort through, than an individual of German, Mexican, Canadian, or Israeli descent.

My brother-in-law, Lawrence, is from Nigeria. My sister-in-law, Fiona, is from Zimbabwe. I have never heard either of them refer to themselves as African-Americans, even though they are more African American than me. Lawrence will proudly tell you, "I'm Nigerian!" Fiona will graciously say, "I'm Zimbabwean!" Because Africa is a continent and not a country, it does me little good to say that I'm African American when attempting to pinpoint my ethnic origin and identity as a black man.

Do we generally and primarily refer to other entire people groups with hyphenated continental descriptions such as

Australian-Americans, South American-Americans, European-Americans, Asian-Americans, Antarctic-Americans, or North American-Americans? No! We refer to them as Canadians, Koreans, Brazilians, Germans, Ugandans, Indians, Israelis, or whatever specific geographical nation they are from. Blacks in America are the only ethnic group of people in the world, inadvertently mislabeled by using the hyphenated name of a continent-nation instead of a specific geographical country of origin. I believe this truth deserves much more thought concerning its implications for victim thinking in black Americans like me.

Traveling As A Black American

As a pastor and preacher of the Gospel of Jesus Christ, international travel is a necessary part of my work. One of the things I enjoy most about traveling is experiencing different cultures, and meeting and interacting with people all over the world. Traveling has enriched my life and broadened my perspective about life and life's circumstances, in a way that isn't possible being confined in my home country.

As I travel internationally, I cannot help but notice the absence of black American travelers abroad. International travelers with darker colored skin are usually citizens of a country located on the continent of Africa. I am comfortable traveling anywhere in the world, but regardless of where I travel, I am always encouraged to hear the distinct accent of another English-speaking American.

At that moment, skin color and ethnicity don't really matter. An instant bond is established based upon one thing–nationalism.

When greeting another American abroad, we are both Americans away from home in a foreign country. Not a black American or a white American–just Americans. Our government doesn't issue one kind of passport for black Americans and another for white Americans–just American passports.

We always greet each other warmly and ask, "Where are you from in the States?" An instant relationship is formed, with a non-verbal understanding that we are patriotically obligated to help each other if needed in a foreign country. Why? Simply because we're citizens of the same country.

My Bus Ride in Uganda

In 2010 I attended a conference in Kampala, Uganda. One of the sessions for the conference was held in a location which necessitated a bus ride to get there. While traveling to our location, I was deeply engaged in a conversation with a fellow American colleague sitting next to me. My colleague asked me a question that led to meaningful and honest dialogue about race issues in America from a Christian faith perspective.

During the conversation, I shared how I learned to process issues pertaining to race in third grade during my time with Mrs. Pitts and my white childhood friends. From that time in my life, I concluded that as a black American, I was to a small degree less empowered concerning my understanding of my ethnic origin when interacting with non-black Americans. I was not disadvantaged intellectually or socio-economically, but I was disadvantaged in terms of my sense of ethnic origin and identity, and belonging to a specific people group from a specific geographical region other than America.

I began to explain to my colleague how black Americans are generally unable to historically trace our heritage back to a specific geographical location. Because of this, we tend to lack a strong sense of ethnic origin, identity, and pride apart from the United States of America. Referring to black Americans as African American is not sufficient in acknowledging the dual national heritage of most American citizens.

For example, Peruvian-Americans, French-Americans, and Korea-Americans are able to physically visit Peru, France, and Korea to more deeply appreciate their heritage, and gain a greater sense of their ethnic origin and identity. They would not only visit the continents of South America, Europe, and Asia, they would visit specific and distinct nations within those continents, each having its own history, traditions, culture, dress code, language, and foods. All variables that help define who they are and what makes them distinct from other ethnic groups, and contributes to their sense of ethnic and national pride.

Even if an *African American* is able to visit the continent of Africa, as I mentioned before, there are approximately fifty-four distinct nations to visit on the continent, each one with its own unique history, traditions, culture, dress code, language, and foods. As a child, I understood that being African American is not specific enough to foster a deep understanding of exactly who we are as an ethnic group of people.

Because of this, I concluded that significant parts of our identity had been lost over time and could not be recovered. As a result, our identity could only be found in heaven–a place where all ethnic groups are equally valuable and equally loved by God. A place where racism and discrimination do not exist. A place where ethnicity could be truly appreciated and celebrated because the same price was paid for all, because all ethnicities are equally valued and loved by God.

A Vision of Three Trees

Just as I was concluding the conversation with my colleague on the bus, I was interrupted by a Christian, Korean-American man sitting next to me. "Excuse me." he said. "I couldn't help overhearing your conversation about black Americans and I would like to share something with you if that's okay." I replied, "Absolutely!"

> "Many years ago I had a vision that concerns black Americans. I never shared the vision with anyone else because it didn't really make sense to me. As a Korean-American, I had no idea what it meant or why God would give it to me. But at this moment, listening to you speak about black Americans, I now understand better what it means, and I believe the vision was meant for you to hear.
>
> I saw a vision of three trees planted in soil. A large hand from heaven grabbed the first tree and attempted to pull it from the soil, but the tree roots were deeply entrenched in the ground. After struggling for some time to pull the tree from the soil, the hand eventually gave up and attempted to uproot the second tree. Although the roots of the second tree gave way more than the first tree, its roots were also deeply entrenched in the ground so the tree could not be removed. After struggling with the second tree, the hand gave up and grabbed the third tree.

> When the hand pulled the third tree it easily and immediately came out of the ground because its roots were very shallow. The roots were covered with soil, so the hand began to violently shake the tree to remove the dirt. After its roots were clean, the hand inverted the tree, and planted the tree upside-down into heaven, and the tree immediately began producing extraordinary fruit in abundance. That third tree represents your people–the Black American people."

The sentiments I carried since my childhood in Tuscaloosa, Alabama concerning black Americans, were confirmed by an unknown Korean-America man, who happened to overhear a random conversation about ethnicity, riding on a bus in Uganda. There was no doubt in my mind that this was a God-ordained moment in time.

While I do realize that many people will disagree with me on this point, in my personal and humble assessment, my own ethnic group–the black American people–still struggle today because of identity crisis and self-worth. I have several reasons for believing that this is painfully true. I'm not referring to all black American individuals on a personal level, as much as I'm referring to our ethnic group taking its proper place among, and in relationship to other ethnic groups in the world.

I see something lacking in the social makeup of the black American community that other ethnic groups seem to possess which is this–a clear sense of ethnic identity, pride, and distinction, which strengthens our collective, ethnic voice in global conversation, our ethnic contribution in global economy, and our ethnic brand in global community. On many occasions, we are not represented at the table. Not because we haven't been invited to the table, but because we're not exactly sure what we bring to the table where value is determined and strategic partnerships are formed.

During my international travels, I've noticed that there seems to be something the Singaporean people believe they have to offer the world. Something unique makes them special and valuable in their own eyes. There seems to be something the German people and Nigerian people have to offer the world. Each of these people groups and others feel at home in their native countries. I'm not so sure black Americans understand or even believe we have something to offer the world and will–something that makes us special and valuable. Something that we are known for and something the world needs.

Considering the traumatic way black Americans historically came to the United States, and our troubled and painful history of racism, discrimination, and oppression, after more than two hundred and forty years, black Americans have never completely felt "at home" in our new home. We still seem to struggle with believing that we are fully accepted, and in some cases we may not be. While we cannot rewrite history or erase these painful memories of the past, I believe the result of these experiences produce a victim mentality within the black American ethnic group, and we especially must initiate intentional intervention to positively alter the course of our future.

Yes, these historical experiences were egregious, unjust, and should be fully condemned. Yes, the residual and lingering effects of them still exist today, even institutionally. Yes, times have changed and tremendous improvements have been made. But unfortunately, the aftermath of victim mentality that stems from being victimized in America still exists. As black Americans, we have to be honest about this if we'll ever be from it.

For those who disagree that victim mentality still plagues black Americans, I would ask, at what point and how did complete healing occur? When did we "get over it?" At what point did black Americans begin to believe that we were fully accepted in America and accept that America is our home? In addition to these, there are many more questions to be asked that pertain to the lingering effects of victim thinking.

Migration Victimization

As a student of the Bible, I see many parallels between the migration of Jacob's son Joseph from Canaan to Egypt, and the migration of black Americans from West Africa to America. While we can never be okay with any form of injustice at any place or any time, injustice is an unfortunate part of our human story. Both the righteous and unrighteous practices of people throughout history have shaped our world. These injustices are always inconceivable in the present, but over time often result in an outcome that is surprisingly beneficial. I believe this to be the case with the slave trade of black, West Africans coming to America, just as it was the case of Joseph being sold as a slave and migrating to Egypt.

One of the greatest examples of a Zero Victim mindset's capacity to turn a bad situation into good, and bring healing and redemption is the story of Joseph we saw earlier. Having suffered betrayal at the hands of his own brothers, Joseph was sold into slavery to Midianite traders who took him from Canaan to Egypt. Without consent or advance notice, Joseph was snatched away from the comforts of his homeland and everything and everyone he loved, and transplanted to a foreign place. As a slave, it is presumed that Joseph suffered many additional, undocumented injustices along the way. As if slavery weren't bad enough, Joseph was later falsely accused, convicted without a trial, and thrown into prison.

At every turn, Joseph seemed to experience even greater injustice, and one day something extraordinary happened. In fulfillment of God's destiny for Joseph's life and His sovereign purposes for the entire nation of Israel, in a moment, Joseph was transferred from prison as a slave, to Pharaoh's palace as the second most powerful man in the world.

After Joseph experienced the traumatic injustice of being ripped from his homeland and sold as a slave, he discovered his destiny in Egypt, not in Canaan. As long as he remained in the comforts of his home in Canaan, his destiny eluded him even though he had a dream about it. In Canaan, he was safe and secure, but not successful. He lived in a place that was familiar to him, but he was not fruitful. At home, Joseph was reverent to God, but somewhat irrelevant to mankind. Through the pain of undeserved injustice, Joseph, for the sake of the future of his people, needed to leave Canaan and migrate to Egypt. We could dare say that the injustice Joseph experienced was a painful blessing in disguise.

Who knows–it may have been that Joseph's love for Canaan was so strong that he would have never voluntarily left to relocate to Egypt, where he was needed. Although God does not orchestrate injustice, He can sovereignly use injustice for His glory, and the ultimate benefit of people groups.

In hindsight, Joseph describes the incident from his perspective:

> *'Thus you shall say to Joseph: "I beg you, please forgive the trespass of your brothers and their sin; for they did evil to you." ' Now, please, forgive the trespass of the servants of the God of your father." And Joseph wept when they spoke to him.*
>
> Genesis 50:17 (NKJV)

> *Joseph said to them, "Do not be afraid, for am I in the place of God? But as for you, you meant evil against me; but God meant it for good, in order to bring it about as it is this day, to save many people alive. Now therefore, do not be afraid; I will provide for you and your little ones." And he comforted them and spoke kindly to them.*
>
> Genesis 50:19-21 (NKJV)

Look Up!

No amount of financial reparations, no apologies, and no protests will ever bring complete healing to black Americans that need it. I believe the healing that is still very much needed, can only come from within, by the grace of God and by the Spirit of God. Healing to such a degree, that if reparations are withheld, if apologies are never spoken, and when protests end, black Americans will occupy a place of fervent faith in God, with a strong sense of identity. And from this place showcase the best of who we are, and offer up our unique ethnic value on a global stage to such a degree, that these aforementioned things would become unnecessary–not unimportant, but unnecessary. With God's help and if we turn to Him, I believe black Americas can indeed rise above any and all injustices with a Zero Victim Mentality and a new attitude!

The principle of the vision of three trees can be applied to any oppressed people group of faith anywhere. I believe God in His goodness shook the dirt clean, and is still shaking the dirt clean from the third tree which represents the black American people. That many of our past struggles, although not precipitated by God, were used by God to cause us to return to faith in Him. We see this precedent set in God's interaction with Israel in the Old Testament. He always used their difficulties as invitations to return to faith in Him, and to receive His salvation and blessing.

I believe it's time for my wonderful black American brothers and sisters to join me in allowing God to plant us in heaven, by returning to faith in God. It is there that we can obtain complete healing individually and collectively, as well as a restored sense of identity and worth as citizens of heaven and members of God's family. It is there and only there that true equality can be obtained. It is there that we are empowered to forgive our enemies and release generational burdens to God. Burdens that are crushing us and are far too great for us to continue to carry.

It is there that we can exchange all forms of victimhood for the victory obtained through faith in Christ. It is there, planted in heaven, that we'll begin to produce the extraordinary fruit we're capable of producing–fruit from which all ethnic groups of the world can eat and be nourished, which will increase our value and contribution to the global economy.

"I believe it's time for my wonderful black American brothers and sisters to join me in allowing God to plant us in heaven, by returning to faith in God."

CHAPTER SIX
Black Man, White Police

Regardless of our ethnicity or political views, we should all be grieved by the senseless and repeated, tragic and fatal incidents we've seen between black men and white police officers. While these incidents are certainly not limited to black men and white cops, those encounters garner more attention than any others, and usually receive more coverage by the mainstream media. The historical volatility that exists between Blacks and Whites in America, makes it so that these incidents quickly become powder kegs of racial tension and a catalyst for social unrest.

Like many other black men, I have been stopped on numerous occasions by white police officers. Each encounter is different. Some are legitimately warranted, while others do seem to be the result of racial profiling. It happens. In some instances, I do believe that a small percentage of hasty, over-zealous white police officers abuse their authority. I also believe that a small percentage of criminally-minded, black men intend to break laws and frequently disregard civil authority. It happens. On both sides, people are people.

While no two sets of circumstances are equivalent, I'd like to share two recent encounters I've had with white police officers, and how I responded with Zero Victim thinking in my attitude and actions toward them.

My Illegal Maneuver

I happen to live in a somewhat exclusive, mostly white, northwest suburb of Chicago. It's a wonderful place to live and raise a family. I describe our town as mostly white, simply because I cannot dogmatically say that we're the only blacks (but it seems like it). If I stay within our community, I can go for weeks and never see another black person or any person of a non-white ethnic group. If I allow my mind to run away with culturally-influenced, unsubstantiated, victim thoughts concerning white people, racism, white privilege, etc., I would be miserable and mentally tormented in the sanctity of my own community.

A few years back, I was driving back home on a two-lane road from taking my children to school. The car ahead of me stopped to make a left turn across oncoming traffic. As I approached the car, I very slowly pulled around it on the right shoulder to continue my drive home. I've seen hundreds of drivers make the same maneuver on this particular road. Local residents know that this happens all the time.

As soon as I passed the car in front of me, I noticed a police car in my rear view mirror with flashing lights. I pulled over to the side of the road and took out my driver's license, insurance, and vehicle registration. When the officer approached my window, I cordially and confidently greeted him while making direct eye contact with him. He greeted me in return. He then asked to see my license, proof of insurance, and vehicle registration. It may seem unnecessary to say this, but my driver's license was valid, my insurance was active, and my registration was up to date.

Some encounters with police can be avoided by simply addressing these matters. I'm intentionally pointing out the validity of my driving credentials, because in so many cases the initial tone of police interaction is set by disobeying the law which says something about my character. My intent to obey or disobey the law tells a policeman what kind of person I am before we ever speak.

People who receive citations for knowingly doing illegal things should not claim victim status. In these cases, the officer's first impression is that they are dealing with an individual who is dishonest, who cannot be trusted, and is somewhat comfortable breaking the law, which immediately creates suspicion. I would imagine that it is natural for an officer to immediately become somewhat edgy when dealing with such people. How can an officer know for sure that this person can be trusted?

When reviewing my documents, the officer noticed that I was a resident of the exclusive town we were in. He proceeded to tell me that the maneuver I made was illegal. While confidently looking him directly in his eyes, I responded by sincerely telling him that I was unaware that the maneuver was illegal and I apologized. My acknowledgment of my wrong and willingness to humbly apologize for it immediately eased any tension between us. He knew he was dealing with an honest black man of integrity. At that moment, I took control of the incident.

At this point, in just a few moments of interaction a few things have already been concretely established. The officer was not suspicious of me. I was compliant and respectful toward him, and not intimidated by him. We were able to clearly and articulately communicate. We could both see that our interaction would not be hostile which I believe determined what would happen next.

The officer again explained that he stopped me because my maneuver was illegal. I genuinely thanked him for informing me of this. He gave me a written warning and began to make conversation with me. "I know most of the residents in this town. How long have you lived here? What do you do?" Among other things, I told him I was a pastor. "A pastor? My family and I need your prayers. And another officer in our department has been diagnosed with terminal cancer, and he and his family could use your prayers as well." I responded, "I most certainly will and thanks for letting me know. I really appreciate the way you guys serve our community. Thank you! If you're ever on our street and have a few moments, stop by and have a cup of coffee." "Thank you pastor. Have a great day." "You too sir."

Sadly, I have never heard a cable news network report on a story like this. In most cases, it seems the only news reported is bad news. My encounter as a black man with this white police officer could have turned out much different. Real-time, intentional decisions were made by both the white police officer and me that contributed to the positive interaction between us. For me, my Zero Victim Mentality guided my interaction with the white police officer, which in turn determined his response to me.

The 5K Incident

Just a few months later, I had a second encounter with a white police officer in the same town, but with a much different narrative. Our home is located next to a nature preserve. There are country roads, three to four miles in length that lead to our neighborhood. These roads are perfectly suited for running and biking. Each year on Thanksgiving Day, our town hosts a 5K run for a significant number of runners. During the run, the residents in the area are very much aware of our need to navigate around the runners to enter and leave our neighborhood.

On Thanksgiving Day, I went to the gym to work out as I do most days. On my way home, when approaching our neighborhood, I encountered several checkpoints set up by the police department to protect the runners, and ensure only residents were permitted to pass. This happens each year and is not unusual. I detest having to refer to skin color and ethnicity in telling this story, but must do so to best recreate the scenario in your mind.

The first checkpoint I encountered was manned by an Asian police officer. He greeted me, "Good morning sir. How are you?" I responded, "I'm fine thank you. And you?" He replied, "Just fine. As you can see, we have runners in the area today. Are you a resident of this community?" "Yes I am." "Great. Then please be careful, drive on the left side of the road, and keep an eye out for the runners. Have a great day." "You as well." I replied.

The second checkpoint I encountered was manned by a black police officer. He also greeted me, "Good morning. Do you live in this community?" "Good morning. And yes I do." "Okay, please drive on the left side of the road and look out for the runners. The run should be over soon." "I certainly will. Thank you officer."

The third checkpoint I came to was manned by a white police officer. In my mind, I anticipated this third checkpoint being uneventful and really unnecessary, considering the fact that I had already passed through two previous checkpoints. As I approached the officer, I rolled down my window and greeted the officer. Without a return greeting and with a stern facial expression, he suspiciously responded, "Do you live here?" I replied, "Yes sir, just around the corner on Lynn Avenue." He then asked, "How far down is Lynn Avenue?" "Two streets on the right." At this point, I concluded that my interaction with the white officer would be nothing like my interaction with the Asian and black police officers.

The white officer continued to interrogate me. "Do you have a driver's license that proves you live on Lynn Avenue?" It was now clear to me that this officer was profiling me and questioning if I *belonged* in this community. I happened to notice that several cars before me passed his checkpoint without being questioned or having to present proof of their residence. I complied with the officer's request and presented my driver's license. He returned my license and authoritatively instructed me, "Drive slow and be careful." He was clearly letting me know that he was in charge.

Those who know me personally can attest that I am not a quick-tempered individual who angers easily. But during this encounter, I could feel something negative quickly rising within me toward this white police officer. Not because of his skin color, but because of his blatant disrespect toward me, and the demeaning use of his civil authority in questioning my character.

Having dealt just moments before with an Asian officer and a black officer from the same department, who both spoke to me with dignity and respect, the contrast of the white officer's condescending tone was crystal clear. Despite the growing tension between us and my emotions being triggered, I decisively chose to apply the universal rule of Zero Victim thinking, which is to act and never react. Because I have preconditioned my mind to immediately rise above and overcome injustice and offense with a proper attitude, it only took a few moments for me to de-escalate the incident, put it in proper perspective, and settle my emotions. Some battles simply aren't worth fighting.

This unfortunate incident shows why Zero Victim mental preconditioning is so vital. Incidents like this can, and unfortunately do turn deadly in a matter of seconds. Like most black people or any oppressed people group, my mind chronicles hundreds of years of injustice and multiple cases of police brutality by white police officers toward black men. If these memories, coupled with my unchecked emotions had taken control of me, and influenced my thinking, speech, behavior, and response toward the white police officer, a hostile and possibly deadly altercation would have been the result. An altercation with a civil authority who carries a badge and a gun, and is authorized to use that gun if he slightly feels threatened in any way, would not have ended well for me.

Without justifying or excusing the white police officer's blatant disrespect toward me and unnecessary profiling of me, engaging him was not safe for me, was not a wise thing to do, and was simply not worth it. Sadly, tens of thousands of black men like me have been in this same scenario and know exactly how it feels. Unfortunately, too many of them are no longer alive to tell about it.

My heart breaks for the numerous tragic and unnecessary deadly incidents between black men and white police officers. Whether we like it or not, we have to allow our courts to decide how to best deal with these incidents according to our rule of law. But for the sake of sparing lives, I wonder how Zero Victim thinking in both black men and white police officers would contribute to better outcomes? I wonder how many lives would have been saved or how many shots would not have been fired. Because of the high probability of imperfect people making instantaneous and erroneous, discretionary decisions in tense moments, I believe it would be well worth our time, effort, and resources to train our officers and people in general in developing a Zero Victim mindset.

The Cardinal Rule of Zero Victim Thinking

The cardinal rule of Zero Victim thinking is to always act intelligently, and never react emotionally. You may be thinking, "That's easier said than done!" However, like many difficult things, it can be done if you are willing to put forth the effort.

During the height of the Black Lives Matter movement, radio and television talk show hosts would often ask me what I thought about the movement. I frequently reiterated this cardinal principle of acting and not reacting, while also agreeing that black lives do matter, even though I was not a supporter of the movement or the organization. As far as I was concerned, yes black lives do matter to me because I'm black. Most importantly, black lives matter to Jesus along with all other lives.

I chose to not endorse the methods or ideologies used by those involved in the movement, but I do understand the movement.

“The cardinal rule of Zero Victim thinking is to always act intelligently, and never react emotionally.”

The movement itself is a cry that resulted from the pain of people who continue to be injured. If you burn your hand on a hot oven door, your natural reaction is not to smile. You'll scream, grimace, or even cry, but you won't respond in a positive way as if you enjoy being burned.

Your future behavior near a hot oven will certainly be defined by your past painful experience. If you become fearful of fire or attempt to pass legislation to ban all hot ovens, victim thinking is evident. An individual with Zero Victim thinking will try to sensibly and logically understand what responsible measures need to be taken to ensure that they are never burned again. Perhaps they need to purchase oven mitts or simply be more careful. This is an example of acting intelligently instead of reacting emotionally.

When I hear of incidents like those between LaQuan McDonald and Jason Van Dyke, George Floyd and Derrick Chauvin, or Jacob Blake Jr. and Rusten Sheshkey, and too many other cases involving white police officers shooting black men, I don't allow myself to react emotionally, even though I'm deeply grieved. Whenever I hear about incidents of racism or allegations against President Trump being a racist, I don't react emotionally. That is when I'm least in control.

Unfortunately, we've had to deal with a few incidents concerning our children to protect them from what seemed to be racist attitudes. I've had to personally deal with matters related to race. But in each case, I always act intelligently instead of reacting emotionally. By doing so, my judgment is not clouded with uncontrollable emotions, and my decision-making is always rational and clear.

Any individual that cannot help reacting emotionally to the inevitable, unfortunate circumstances of life, will never live in peace and will always be easily controlled. Zero Victim thinking is the key to living in what the Bible refers to as the peace of God that passes understanding (Philippians 4:7).

CHAPTER SEVEN
Victim Thinking Has Infected Society

An undesirable effect that affects a society, will eventually infect that society permanently. An infection is always associated with some form of contamination that is harmful and often results in death. I believe our current society is sick and is dying a slow death because of victim thinking. This infectious disease is also highly contagious and is rapidly spreading in the hearts and minds of those who have not built up strong immunity against it.

Victim Mentality is Rapidly Spreading

As I observe our nation and pay careful attention to current events and how people respond to them, I see victim mentality rapidly spreading across America and increasing with each subsequent generation. Victimization is being woven into the fabric of our society. Our educational, entertainment, political, and economic systems are increasingly being laced with victim thinking. The more victim thinking spreads it is being normalized–the more it is normalized, it is also being politicized and then institutionalized.

Systems are being constructed to promote and protect victim thinking. Politicians are building political platforms that cater to, and pander those who have embraced an ideology of victim thinking. They often highlight and play the victim card to gain votes from people who believe they have been victimized, even if their claims are unsupported and unsubstantiated. The people need not prove that they are really victims. They only need to claim to be victims based upon their personal feelings.

The campaign platform of politicians who exploit victim thinking usually includes promises to end the wars on women, gays, blacks, poor people, immigrants, and others. Each political election becomes more cantankerous than the last. Once elected, these politicians promote and advocate for their legislation of victimization to become law, while declaring themselves to be "champions for the American people." Many of them spend their political tenure "fighting" to alleviate the victimizations they convinced people to believe.

This politicized form of subjective, victim thinking eventually functions as a catch-all ideology in determining what is, and is not a hate crime. I am sad to say that legitimate hate crimes do happen and I vehemently condemn those who commit them. Such individuals must be punished to the full extent of the law.

“Spiritual law is the father and moral law is the mother that conceive and give birth to the offspring of civil law.”

But in this context, when referring to hate crimes, I am speaking to how widespread victim thinking has contributed to the redefinition of what is considered to be a hate crime. In today's America, it seems that anyone who simply feels or perceives in any way that they are disliked or disagreed with, is the legitimate victim of a hate crime. The new social paradigm is referred to as *cancel culture*. More and more, it seems that civil law is being shaped and redefined by subjective feelings based upon victim thinking, instead of the objective fundamentals of spiritual and moral law.

Three Kinds of Law

Much of the confusion and division we see developing in society can be traced back to a lack of understanding concerning how law holistically works. Civil law was never intended to exist apart from spiritual law and moral law. Spiritual law is the father and moral law is the mother that conceive and give birth to the offspring of civil law. Civil law cannot exist or support itself any more than a new born baby can exist and support itself without its father and mother. Alone, it is helpless, defenseless, and will quickly die. The more we ignore or dismiss the significant necessity of spiritual and moral law, the more we place unreasonable expectations on politicians to define our way of living through their personal, subjective, flawed, and humanistic interpretations of what civil law is or is not.

To a righteous, spiritual, and moral people, civil law is somewhat inconsequential. Penalties for murder as determined by civil law are only relevant and necessary when people are no longer governed by spiritual and moral law. Because spiritual and moral people don't kill, a civil law that makes murder a crime is unnecessary. Together, spiritual and moral law are much more effective in righteously governing a society than civil law could ever be. People capable of policing themselves internally by spiritual and moral law, don't need to be policed externally by civil law.

Spiritual law is law that comes from God and is given to mankind. In the Bible, in Exodus chapter 20, God gave Israel His spiritual laws, better known as the Decalogue or Ten Commandments:

1. You shall have no other gods before Me.
2. You shall make no idols.
3. You shall not take the name of the Lord your God in vain.
4. Remember the Sabbath day to keep it holy.
5. Honor your father and your mother.
6. You shall not murder.
7. You shall not commit adultery.
8. You shall not steal.
9. You shall not bear false witness against your neighbor.
10. You shall not covet.

It completely baffles me that some self-righteous people and politicians have declared these spiritual laws given by God Himself, to be a violation of civil law and have declared them to be unconstitutional. What arrogance and pride! How can any human conclude that they know better than God?

When believed and obeyed, these timeless and spiritual laws are designed to write moral law on the hearts of people. Because of them, people can now intrinsically know the difference between right and wrong without the government's involvement. By our own conscience, shaped by God's spiritual law, we know internally that murder, stealing, and adultery is wrong.

Because of moral law within our conscience, defined by God's spiritual law, civil law is nothing more than a documented footnote and reminder of spiritual and moral law. Civil law also serves to establish a common denominator for acceptable social conduct which allows people to co-exist in community. Civil law prescribes accepted consequences beforehand for those who break spiritual or moral law. Of the three, we see that civil law is the lowest form of law. Sadly, we're witnessing the absolute and total rejection of spiritual law in America, which is resulting in the rapid deterioration of moral law, and the subjective redefinition of morality in our society.

From "So Help Me God!" To "God Don't Help Me!"

It's always interesting to see politicians and most notably our Presidents take their oath of office by placing their hand on a Holy Bible, and conclude their oath by saying, "So help me God." With respect, whenever I see this, I sometimes want to shout, "You're lying!" Some of them lie about their intent to keep their oath while being placed under oath! How can this be? It happens because they have little or no regard for spiritual law, and they themselves either disregard moral law, or have determined for themselves what is and is not moral.

Many politicians enact policies that violate what's written in the same Bible they place their hand on when being sworn into office. So help me God? God certainly doesn't help them disobey His Word. At the very least, the gesture of swearing on the Bible

"Sadly, we're witnessing the absolute and total rejection of spiritual law in America, which is resulting in the rapid deterioration of moral law, and the subjective redefinition of morality in our society."

and entreating God for help is an acknowledgement that God gave us spiritual law contained in the Scriptures, and that moral law is needed to govern righteously and uphold civil law.

As our nation drifts away from God and rejects His absolute, spiritual law, moral law increasingly becomes relative, corrupt, and distorted. In the absence of spiritual law, moral law is easily and conveniently redefined to best suit the self-centered, humanistic, carnal, and political interests of people. What's moral today could be considered immoral tomorrow, based upon the extent of victim thinking that exists in society. For example, abortion and sodomy have historically been considered immoral and thus illegal, but today they are considered to be moral and are legal. What changed? Widespread victim thinking has changed the narrative concerning these vital issues, making them about rights under civil law instead of righteousness under moral law.

God's spiritual law concerning these immoral practices has been disregarded. With spiritual law removed, civil laws have been amended to accommodate people who reject spiritual law and desire to define their own morality. Whenever these individuals feel victimized by those who disagree with their actions, additional hate crime laws are called for to pave the way for the criminal prosecution of their opponents. This is how widespread, social victim thinking is purported through legislation.

Self-proclaimed liberal politicians have entrenched themselves in opposing Biblical moral laws, and intend to implement their version of civil laws to govern our nation, and it all began with the dismissal of God's absolute spiritual law. Until our political leaders are willing to humble themselves to return to God's spiritual law, they will remain irreconcilably divided

"What's moral today could be considered immoral tomorrow, based upon the extent of victim thinking that exists in society."

when it comes to morality. By only considering civil law, our present two-party political system is incapable of re-discovering the common denominator of God's Word, in answering the great questions of our day concerning healthcare, racial reconciliation, justice, immigration, abortion, sexual orientation, and others.

Victim Thinking Influence Politics

As far back as I can remember, the narrative that black people are supposed to be Democrats because the Democratic party helps black people has existed in my mind. I'm not exactly sure where it originated. It was always just there since my childhood. This is an example of how powerful indoctrination and the politicization of victim thinking can be.

As a black American, if I remain uninformed and believe this narrative to be true, I will automatically vote Democrat along party lines, regardless of the character and beliefs of the candidates or the policies they represent. I would always feel obligated to vote Democrat simply because I believe they will help black people. This is called identity politics. My uniformed vote would in turn further ensure that civil law would continue to reinforce victim thinking, and be reinforced by it.

Free At Last!

Zero Victim thinking freed me from the mental controls and emotional influence of any political party. I don't need any politician to represent my struggles and alleviate my problems as a black man because I'm not a victim. I don't need their help–they need mine. That's how they get elected into office. It really

"Whenever spiritual and moral law is lacking in government, corruption is widespread and nations eventually topple."

saddens me to see politicians simultaneously pushing victim thinking along with 'Get Out and Vote' campaigns.

God's spiritual law to me, shapes and defines moral law within me, to the point I don't really need civil law to govern me. As a spiritual and moral citizen, it is my duty and responsibility to help hold our government accountable for being righteous. We must never forget that people make governments. When governments begin to make people, disaster will soon follow.

We seem to have lost this conviction in America. More and more, civil law from the government is shaping the lives of people, instead of spiritual and moral law in people shaping the government. Whenever spiritual and moral law is lacking in government, corruption is widespread and nations eventually topple.

All humanitarian crises and social problems are the result of broken spiritual and moral laws, and cannot be resolved using civil law alone. We deceive ourselves into thinking and expecting the government to solve these issues with more legislation and better civil laws. Each time a mass shooting occurs, politicians call for more gun laws, but never call for penitence of hearts, evidenced by a return to spiritual and moral law. Civil law is incapable of acknowledging the sin of destroying those who are image-bearers of God.

The cycle continues. Congress legislates more civil laws. The Supreme Court tries more cases to better interpret civil laws, and our nation continues to decline spiritually and morally. As a result, we believe we need bigger and better government, with more programs and services, to solve problems associated with governing a less spiritual and less moral people. In due time, the system is destined to implode. This is what happens when victim thinking infects a nation at its core.

CHAPTER EIGHT

Examples of Zero Victim Thinkers

One of the historical black American figures I respect most is Booker T. Washington. By the turn of the 20th century, Booker Taliaferro Washington had become an adviser to multiple presidents of the United States. Through his influential writings and captivating speeches, Washington had become the most prominent leader in the black American community, and represented the new black social elite.

Booker T. was burdened to do whatever in God's name he could do to save the next generation of black Americans from the mental and social burdens carried by the previous generation. Born a slave on a plantation in Franklin County, Virginia, he was never certain of the exact place and date of his birth. Booker T. never knew his father's name, although his father was rumored to be a white man from a nearby plantation. Even so, Booker T. was not bitter toward his father, and believed him to be a victim of the institution the nation had forced upon him.

In his writings, Booker T. describes being raised in miserable, desolate, and discouraging surroundings. Like any other human born into such conditions, Booker T. could easily justify victimization in his own thinking. He received no schooling as a slave, yet he was known to be forward-thinking in his perspectives in life. Despite the hardships black Americans faced, Booker T. embraced a Zero Victim mindset and believed Blacks could rise above every challenge they faced. Here's an example of his forward-thinking perspective and intent to act intelligently and not react emotionally:

> *To teach the Negro to read, whether English, or Greek, or Hebrew, butters no parsnips. To make the Negro work, that is what his master did in one way and hunger has done in another; yet both these left Southern life where they found it. But to teach the Negro to do skillful work, as men of all the races that have risen have worked,–responsible work, which IS education and character; and most of all when Negroes so teach Negroes to do this that they will teach others with a missionary zeal that puts all ordinary philanthropic efforts to shame,–this is to change the whole economic basis of life and the whole character of a people.*[1]

Booker Washington believed in taking personal responsibility for the future by taking action. It was his belief that education, work, and character would cause Blacks to rise socially and

[1] Washington, Booker T.. Up from Slavery: an autobiography. Kindle Edition.

become more economically independent. As Blacks became more economically independent, they would then become a significant part of Southern life, forcing Whites to recognize and respect them. After all, during this time Blacks possessed the entrepreneurial know-how to successfully produce tobacco, cotton, and sugarcane, which represented the backbone of the southern economy.

While still a slave, Booker T. writes about the development of the Civil War. He recalled no bitter feelings by him or Blacks around him toward white people, even though much of the white population were away fighting a war to keep Blacks enslaved. On the contrary, he recounts feeling emotions of sorrow and sympathy when hearing the news of the death of one of his young slave masters and two other Whites being severely injured in the war. When white men went off to the war, it was oftentimes their slaves that protected their wives and children, even defending them with their lives.

Contrary to what we tend to believe or what modern social narratives would suggest, in Booker's case, he and those around him were not at all embittered as slaves, and did not embrace or endorse victim thinking.

> *As a rule, not only did the members of my race entertain no feelings of bitterness against the Whites before and during the war, but there are many instances of Negroes tenderly caring for their former masters and mistresses who for some reason have become poor and dependent since the war. I know of instances where the former masters of slaves have for years*

been supplied with money by their former slaves to keep them from suffering.[2]

I have long since ceased to cherish any spirit of bitterness against the Southern White people on account of the enslavement of my race.[3]

While studying Booker T's writings, I was ecstatic to read that more than one hundred years ago, he shared my perspective about the forced migration of Blacks from Africa to America, similar to the forced migration of Joseph from Canaan to Egypt.

Having once got its tentacles fastened on to the economic and social life of the Republic, it was no easy matter for the country to relieve itself of the institution. Then, when we rid ourselves of prejudice, or racial feeling, and look facts in the face, we must acknowledge that, notwithstanding the cruelty and moral wrong of slavery, the ten million Negroes inhabiting this country, who themselves or whose ancestors went through the school of American slavery, are in a stronger and more hopeful condition, materially, intellectually, morally, and religiously, than is true of an equal number of Black people in any other portion of the globe.[4]

This I say, not to justify slavery–on the other hand, I condemn it as an institution, as we all know that in America it was established for selfish and financial reasons, and not from a missionary motive–but to call attention to a fact, and

---

[2] Washington, Booker T.. Up from Slavery: an autobiography (p. 5). Kindle Edition.
[3] Washington, Booker T.. Up from Slavery: an autobiography (p. 6). Kindle Edition.
[4] Washington, Booker T.. Up from Slavery: an autobiography (p. 6). Kindle Edition.

to show how Providence so often uses men and institutions to accomplish a purpose.[5]

By now you can see why I respect Booker T. Washington as a revolutionary Zero Victim thinker and pioneer of his day. His comments are not to be interpreted as justification for the injustice of slavery, but to recognize the sovereign hand of God at work through both the acceptable and unacceptable behaviors of people. To further your study of his Zero Victim thinking, during a time that was much more difficult for black Americans than today, I suggest you read Booker T. Washington's autobiography entitled, *Up from Slavery*.

Queen Esther Was A Zero Victim Thinker

In the days of multiple feminist movements intended to empower women and address gender inequality issues, I encourage women of faith who desire to become Zero Victim thinkers to carefully study the life of Queen Esther. Along with many stories of the historical struggles of the Jewish people, I glean tremendous wisdom and inspiration from the story of Esther.

From all conceivable angles, Hadassah, also known as Esther, experienced extreme injustice and victimization. Her family had been exiled from Jerusalem to Babylon by King Nebuchadnezzar. After the death of her parents, Esther was orphaned, but later adopted and raised by her cousin, Mordecai.

---

[5] Washington, Booker T.. Up from Slavery: an autobiography (pp. 6-7). Kindle Edition.

As a result of the king's decree, Esther, along with many other young women experienced the injustice of being forcefully taken into the king's harem as a concubine. Amazingly, despite these most unfortunate circumstances, Esther sought to serve the king obediently and faithfully, without any outward indication of offense. The Bible records how the king's custodian was highly impressed with Esther and showed her great favor. Because of her positive attitude, he treated her much better than the other women, and moved Esther to the best place in the house.

The king's objective was to marry a young woman who would be pleasing to him. I believe if Esther had embraced victim thinking, while complaining of the injustice she experienced, she would have quickly been disqualified as a candidate to be chosen by the king. Please listen to me! I am in no way endorsing the sick and detestable practice of women being subject to the modern-day equivalent of the "casting couch" culture in entertainment. My point is to highlight Esther's decision to not respond as a victim, but choose to rise above the injustice she was experiencing with a new attitude. Let's not forget that God chose her to be an example to us all in Scripture.

Esther's Zero Victim Mindset enabled her to think critically and strategically when it mattered most. When the time came for her to approach the king, Esther didn't take the items for beautification she preferred. She asked the king's custodian to advise her concerning what the king preferred to gain his favor. The end result was that the king loved Esther more than all the other women, and she obtained grace and favor in his sight to become queen. The king even proclaimed a holiday in the provinces in Esther's honor.

"Esther's Zero Victim Mindset enabled her to think critically and strategically when it mattered most."

Queen Esther Endures Racism

Because of his hatred for Esther's Jewish cousin Mordecai, Haman, an unrighteous, racist, appointed prince, decided that he would destroy all Jewish people because of Mordecai. This was blatant racism that would result in genocide if Haman had his way. Haman deceptively convinced the king that the Jewish people were lawless and a threat to the king, and therefore should be destroyed. The king ignorantly agreed. Haman's vitriol immediately escalated into overt persecution of the Jewish people. Letters were sent by couriers into all the king's provinces to destroy, kill, and annihilate all Jews, both young and old, little children and women, in one day. By the king's decree, this letter became law. A civil rights movement was desperately needed if the Jewish people would survive.

Although Esther was now queen, she was not among the seven princes who had special access to the king's presence to approach him, and therefore, she risked death if she approached the king uninvited to address this heinous crime. Upon hearing the law to annihilate his people, Mordecai sends word to Esther to approach the king to make supplication and plead for the salvation of the Jews. Esther retorts by reminding Mordecai that a law was in place that anyone who approached the king's presence without being called would be put to death, except the one to whom the king held out his golden scepter. And Esther had not been called.

In his reply, Mordecai reminds Esther that she too is a Jew and would also be destroyed with the others if she did not intervene. Esther finally concedes and decides that she would approach the king, even if it meant her death. When Esther approached the king, he not only spared her life, the king promised to grant her

"By being gracious, respectful, wise, and a Zero Victim thinker, Esther chose a new attitude that enabled and empowered her to single-handedly save her entire people group."

request up to half his kingdom, even before hearing what she had to say. That's the potential power of Zero Victim thinking!

Esther eventually saved her people from genocide, and to this day is highly regarded, remembered, and celebrated during the Jewish holiday of Purim. By being gracious, respectful, wise, and a Zero Victim thinker, Esther chose a new attitude that enabled and empowered her to single-handedly save her entire people group. I believe Esther's life and Zero Victim attitude toward extreme injustice, is a case study for any would-be deliverer on the power of Zero Victim thinking.

Lessons From The Jewish People

Today, we hear so much about the historical and present-day struggles of black Americans. Every few years, we hear calls for reparations to remedy the historical disadvantages and adverse effects of what many believe to be white privilege in America. As a Christian, black American man who's familiar with the Scriptures, I often think of the Jewish people. We can easily argue that there has not been a more oppressed people group in the history of civilization. I have observed a few admirable characteristics about the Jewish people that I believe are vital in the development of a Zero Victim Mindset.

Whether they consider themselves to be cultural, orthodox, religious, or ethnic Jews, the Jewish people possess a very strong sense of identity that can be traced back to Abraham, the father of the Jewish people. They seem to carry a strong sense of self-worth, which empowers them to know their value in the world and to the world, as well as what distinct contributions their people group can make in our global society. Despite their past oppression

"As a Christian, black American man who's familiar with the Scriptures, I often think of the Jewish people."

and extreme victimizations, the Jewish people have embraced a protective Zero Victim philosophy and attitude of "Never again!"

Having decided that historical injustice, oppression, and victimization will never happen to them again, they work together as a people group to maintain and increase their overall strength. As a result, the Jewish people possess great wealth and have gained widespread influence in every sector of society. Because God does not show partiality, I believe He can bless black Americans and any other people group to prosper and thrive, just as He has blessed the Jewish people, when Zero Victim thinking is wholeheartedly embraced.

CHAPTER NINE

Five Steps to Begin the Mental Process: Prepare Yourself!

I have been privileged to mentor many individuals over the years. I would often encourage them with this thought–preparation and courage are essential to survival, when living in a hostile world. Imagine if an astronaut entered space without the proper spacesuit and equipment, and was mentally unprepared. He or she would stand little chance of surviving in that hostile environment.

We tend to focus on preparation to obtain the material things we need in life, such as homes, cars, and money, but often fail to prepare ourselves mentally and emotionally. Essential mental and emotional preparation helps you obtain mental freedom, which will permit you to better protect yourself from victimization in a hostile environment.

It is most unfortunate when any person is bullied. But in that situation, only one solution exists and the victim has only one option. If you absolutely cannot avoid a fight with a bully, you must do everything you can to prepare yourself to fight the bully and win! Because life attempts to bully each of us, a few basic skills are necessary to minimally prepare yourself to fight the bully and win!

Know Your Environment

Success in any setting begins with a careful analysis of your environment. If you have been camping or hiking, you know the importance of determining your exact location as well as directional orientation. Furthermore, consulting maps and the weather forecast better prepares you for the adventure ahead. The degree to which you prepare determines if your adventure will be delightful or deadly.

As a corporate executive, I discovered how making sudden organizational changes without first thoroughly assessing the environment is unwise. Assessing your environment first includes identifying your friends and foes. Keep in mind that your enemies are not always people, but sometimes ideals or even circumstances. Each of us must wrestle with issues in our immediate environment over which we have little or no control.

In some cases, we were born into predetermined and pre-existing conditions. Sometimes we think of these conditions as the "cards" we were dealt. None of us had control over when we were born or who our parents were. We did not choose our ethnicity

"Essential mental and
emotional preparation helps
you obtain mental freedom,
which will permit you
to better protect yourself
from victimization in
a hostile environment."

or gender. By default, we were subject to the choices our parents made (good or bad) and were born into an environment defined by them.

Many people never learn to take control of their environment early in life, and find themselves subject to their environment in their latter years. They may stay on a job they don't like or live in a neighborhood they don't prefer. They may remain attached to a community of people who don't have their best interest at heart, or find themselves in close relationships with people they never chose to befriend. Each of these environments is a potential hazard. Some of these individuals refuse to make tough choices, blame others, and take on a lifetime of victim thinking. Other individuals are repeatedly victimized throughout their entire life because of their unwillingness to change.

You can assess and know your environment by simply utilizing SWOT Analysis to identify immediate *strengths*, *weaknesses*, *opportunities*, and *threats* around you. To avoid becoming a victim, you must take this critical step in preparing yourself mentally, by identifying hostilities in your immediate environment.

Know Yourself

In addition to carefully assessing your external environment, you must also assess your internal environment. I have taken many personality assessment tests. I don't rely on them to tell me who I am, but use them to affirm and clarify what I already know to be true about myself.

In a hostile world, a critical and necessary skill is knowing both who you are and who you are not. I once heard a preacher comment that an ear will forever be frustrated as long as he is enrolled in nose school, and will be disheartened by his inability to adequately smell. But if he attends ear school, he experiences the joy and glory of fulfilling his purpose of hearing, which no other body part can do as well as he can.

Knowing yourself gives you the greatest chance to avoid becoming a victim. Analyzing yourself will help you better identify internal hazards and weaknesses that contribute to victimization. Sometimes hostilities are not around you, but are within you. I humbly try to honestly assess and acknowledge my own strengths and weaknesses, which helps me navigate a successful path through a hostile world.

Your family's financial position, religious beliefs, and ethnic culture all played a significant part in defining your childhood and brought you to where you presently are. Take time to carefully consider these pre-existing conditions. Your predetermined environment shaped your mentality, your values, and your beliefs. These factors molded your behavioral tendencies during the most formative years of your life. As a result, you are hardwired to see and believe certain things as established norms.

You can significantly decrease your probability of victimization by carefully analyzing your pre-existing conditions and examining your past experiences. Ask yourself, "What values and beliefs shaped my mentality as a child? What past experiences cause me to think the way that I think?" Because your internal environment is the sum total of your past, you must take the necessary time to thoroughly unpack it and strive to better know yourself.

Secure The Necessary Assistance You Need

The fact that you are reading this book proves that you already understand the importance and value of getting help. You may have heard of certain people being referred to as "self-made" individuals. I believe "self-made" is a misnomer. Most everyone who will achieve success will do so with the support of many people. No one can succeed alone. Hear the wise words of King Solomon:

> *Two people are better off than one, for they can help each other succeed. If one person falls, the other can reach out and help. But someone who falls alone is in real trouble. Likewise, two people lying close together can keep each other warm. But how can one be warm alone? A person standing alone can be attacked and defeated, but two can stand back-to-back and conquer. Three are even better, for a triple-braided cord is not easily broken* (Ecclesiastes 4:9-12).

King Solomon comments that the mutually beneficial and combined efforts of two people are better than one person attempting to succeed alone. If one of them happens to fall (which we are all prone to do in life), the other person is there to help. Note how King Solomon makes reference to an individual being attacked and defeated. Whether spiritually, emotionally, or mentally, you can expect vicious attacks to happen in a hostile world. We must constantly defend ourselves against victimizations in life. If we stand alone, we will certainly be defeated.

"Analyzing yourself will help you better identify internal hazards and weaknesses that contribute to victimization."

I wrote this book to become a close ally to you as you defend yourself against the enemy of victim thinking. Similar to the athletic coach who studies the opposing team, devises strategies, and motivates his players to win, consider me to be your Zero Victim coach. I believe in you and desire to help you obtain the mental victory needed to revolutionize your life and enable you to win!

Victim mentality is not something that any of us can defeat alone. Doing so requires right information and support from other individuals who understand the importance of eliminating victim thinking. We must also find individuals to whom we can make ourselves accountable. At times, we will all be tempted to momentarily revert back to victim mentality. Therefore, we must endeavor to secure the assistance we need on an ongoing basis.

Precondition Your Mind

Living in a hostile world also requires mental toughness. The purpose of this book is to show you how to *rise above offense and injustice with a new attitude*. I have discovered that attitude in life determines altitude in life. People can only go as high as their attitude will take them. Even before circumstances happen, winning and losing starts in the mind. I want to give you the tools necessary to overcome life's challenges even before they arise. You can develop your mind in such a way that negative circumstances will never again happen *to you* because you anticipated them beforehand, and were adequately prepared mentally and emotionally for their arrival.

Preconditioning your thoughts will strengthen your mind to the point that unfortunate circumstances cannot "break" you. If

“I have discovered that attitude in life determines altitude in life. People can only go as high as their attitude will take them.”

permitted, fear will attempt to grip your mind and paralyze you, while tormenting you in the process. Mental preparedness is essential for resisting fear and maintaining your winning resolve when dealing with difficult circumstances in life.

By preconditioning your mind to expect the unexpected, you position yourself to act but never react, thus avoiding becoming a victim of stress and anxiety through mental preparation. Lack of knowledge can be destructive. Therefore, you must arm yourself with the best information available, and wisely use that information to create a strategy to avoid and overcome victimizations in life.

Envision Your Victory

Finally, to succeed in a hostile world, you must envision yourself as a victor and not a victim through the eyes of faith. When faced with challenging situations in the past, I attempted to determine the next immediate step to be taken to successfully move forward. This method proved to be unproductive because my perspective was too small to even gauge the full scope of the problem I was attempting to solve. I eventually grew wiser and changed my approach.

Now when I'm faced with challenging situations, I don't look for the immediate next step. Instead, I carefully envision the desired outcome of my success in its entirety. We commonly refer to this as *seeing the big picture*. I have trained my mind to fast forward to the hypothetical and best case scenario conclusion of the situation. Then I work my way backwards to my present position by exercising reverse decision making. As a result, I never see myself as a victim of my circumstances, but as a victor

“By preconditioning your mind to expect the unexpected, you position yourself to act but never react, thus avoiding becoming a victim of stress and anxiety through mental preparation.”

who has already overcome my circumstances, which allows me to develop a clear exit strategy. This mental exercise of envisioning your victory will empower you to maximize time and minimize pitfalls, by allowing you to distinguish what actions are necessary and unnecessary as you strive to improve your circumstances. Having envisioned the end result, you must then adopt a *can-do, will-do,* and *must-do* attitude.

Each of these five steps are needed to defend against becoming a victim and to prepare you for the fight that life will most certainly pick with you. Remember, life is a bully! Challenges are inevitably coming your way. But you can prepare yourself for them by developing a mentality that makes you invincible no matter what circumstances you face in this hostile world.

CHAPTER TEN
Responding to Injustice Is a Skill

As more and more people develop a Zero Victim Mentality, we will stand a much better chance of improving our society. Why? Because those individuals will be empowered to appropriately react to injustice. Each time injustice occurs in society, more people assume the victim role. As tragedies become greater and happen more frequently, victim mentality becomes pervasive within our culture and further defines our nation. I'm afraid that America has become a nation filled with people who suffer from victim mentality.

Whenever injustice occurs in our nation on a large scale, public outcry ensues. The news anchors engage and present the tragedy as *breaking news*. Each network claims to have the most trusted information. People take to social media, posting their multifaceted opinions about the crisis. Hashtags are immediately created, and the social media sparring begins. This phenomenon is the greatest promoter of victim thinking in today's culture.

Politicians denounce injustice publicly while finding a way to blame the opposite political party as being somehow responsible for the incident. The tragedy immediately becomes a potential platform to secure votes for the next election. Empty promises are made to make the necessary changes to prevent the tragedy from happening again. Eventually, news of the incident no longer sustains high enough ratings and is soon forgotten publicly, but the victims' lives continue to be impacted.

In chapter three we examined some of the unfortunate outcomes of living in a hostile world. We saw how victims are potentially created from the pre-existing conditions they are born into, from the messages they received as a child, or from their unfortunate relationships with others. We usually respond to victimization by assigning blame to others, and confronting who or what we believe to be the source. Seeking to stop injustice at its point of origin is certainly necessary to ultimately end victimization, but this action represents only one half of the solution and attempts to solve the problem from only one perspective.

Understanding Zero Victim Mentality Through Baseball

To the best of our ability, we must earnestly attempt to prevent tragedies from happening, but we cannot stop there. That's not enough. By only attempting to prevent injustice from happening and responding to it when it does, we will always find

"I'm afraid that America
has become a nation filled
with people who suffer
from victim mentality."

ourselves chasing problems and managing the fallout of injustice. This approach alone will not eliminate victimization.

Trying to stop injustice by only attempting to prevent its occurrence is similar to having a one-sided coin. Both sides of the coin are necessary for it to be considered valid currency. If striving to stop injustice were the "heads" side of the coin, the "tails" side would be preparing ourselves mentally to deal with injustice by anticipating it before it even happens.

To better understand the benefit of anticipating injustice, think of the relationship between a pitcher and catcher in baseball. From the catcher's perspective, it is not a matter of if, but when the next pitch will be thrown. He understands that a 100-mph fastball can be life-threatening if it isn't managed properly. To lessen the possibility of him being seriously injured or even killed, the catcher wears the proper equipment to protect himself.

Once the catcher puts on his protective gear, his primary objective shifts from protecting himself to now managing the life-threatening projectile soon coming his way. His ability to concentrate on catching a pitch comes only after he has first obtained peace of mind by protecting himself from personal injury. Once properly protected, he squats into position, extends his mitt, and patiently waits for the pitch to arrive. Because of the velocity of the pitch, the catcher cannot prepare to receive the pitch after it is thrown. He must place himself in a posture of readiness to receive the pitch before the ball leaves the pitcher's hand.

You must think of injustice and victimization as a 100-mph fastball coming your way. Similar to a catcher's posture of readiness, a Zero Victim Mentality equips you to protect

"I believe that people are highly intelligent and are capable of thinking their way through unfortunate events without having to react emotionally and uncontrollably."

yourself from the danger coming your way, and to then catch it successfully. Once you mentally prepare yourself to address injustice beforehand, you will be no more surprised by its arrival than a catcher is by a pitcher's fastball.

Sometimes a catcher is not even sure what kind of pitch will be thrown. Some pitches may arrive as a fastball, while others will arrive as a curveball, a slider, or changeup. A great catcher must be ready to receive anything. Likewise, a Zero Victim thinker protects and readies himself or herself to receive any form of injustice, whether it arrives as an insult, disrespect, offense, a sexist remark, or even a racial slur. In each case, when the life-threatening injustice gets thrown their way, no injury occurs. It is simply caught and stopped.

Our Responsibility to Improve Our Reaction

I believe that we can collectively do a much better job of conditioning the minds of people to develop the mental toughness necessary to better deal with offenses and negative circumstances that come their way. I believe that people are highly intelligent and are capable of thinking their way through unfortunate events without having to react emotionally and uncontrollably. By changing your mentality to deal with injustice before it happens, you will be ready for it, if and when it transpires.

This will undoubtedly lessen the catastrophic fallout that happens when something inappropriate or offensive happens, which unfortunately will always be the case. We must not only seek to instill greater respect and sensitivity into the heart and mind of the offender, but also seek to toughen the minds of the offended to take more responsibility for their response in better

"Injustice in any case is certainly a tragedy, but sometimes people's reaction to the injustice outdoes the injustice itself."

handling the offense. Injustice in any case is certainly a tragedy, but sometimes people's reaction to the injustice outdoes the injustice itself. A person's reaction to a crime can also be criminal or even more egregious than the original crime.

More and more, I am greatly troubled by the reactions I see to unfortunate events. I've noticed that when people disagree with an individual's opinions or perspectives, that individual often reacts by demonizing and attacking them, labeling them as bigots, racist, homophobic, anti-women, anti-poor, etc., all because they simply disagree with their opinion or hold a different point of view. These reactions gave rise to what's now known as *cancel culture*, which is an attempt to completely silence any differing points of view. Zero Victim thinking is needed because it cancels *cancel culture.*

When this reaction repeats throughout a society, offense becomes greatly amplified and a culture of victimization emerges. One group is said to be warring against another. Think about it. Any war that occurs within a nation's border is a civil war. This disunity will only weaken that nation to the point that it will eventually collapse. Jesus speaks to this truth in stating, "Every kingdom divided against itself is brought to desolation, and every city or house divided against itself will not stand" (Matthew 12:25, NKJV).

As a nation, we fail to acknowledge this type of retaliatory response as incorrect and unacceptable. We seem to cater to an individual's right to respond in an inappropriate manner, instead of challenging them to respond in a respectful and tactful way. When we cater to an individual's right to respond disrespectfully, we encourage the prevalence of victim mentality throughout society.

Our Reaction to Injustice Matters

Several years ago, Don Sterling, owner of the Los Angeles Clippers' professional basketball team, was unknowingly recorded making racist comments about African-American people. The Supreme Court made a controversial ruling in favor of the religious values of the Green family, owners and founders of the Hobby Lobby Corporation. Celebrity chef Paula Deen came under fire for allegedly confessing to using the " N" word. Former Mozilla CEO Brendan Eich resigned in the wake of a rising boycott against him related to his position on gay rights.

Chick-fil-A CEO Dan Cathy, a self-described evangelical Christian, came under fire concerning his views about traditional marriage. Business owners David and Jason Benham were at the center of a controversy regarding their conservative views on abortion and gay marriage. These are just a few of the innumerable stories that developed from verbal comments considered to be offensive acts of injustice.

I don't intend here to take a position concerning the incidents in which these individuals were allegedly involved. I only desire to call our collective attention to how we respond to these incidents and so many others. As I previously mentioned, seeking to reprimand these individuals represents only one side of the coin. The other side concerns how their accusers reacted to what they were accused of doing.

The Power of Media Affects Our Response

In our culture of instant access to global information, media greatly affects our response to injustice. We must realize that for every incident that occurs in our nation, executives in media make decisions concerning what to report and what to ignore. Whoever those individuals are, they possess tremendous power to control social narratives and public reactions.

Once the press decides which injustices to cover or not cover, they also decide how to present the information often referred to as "spin." Commentary, interviews, and pictures are all carefully chosen to paint a specific picture about the injustice reported with the intent to influence the sentiments of those viewing and listening. I am not suggesting that information about injustice should ever be withheld or that injustice should be overlooked. I consider failing to responsibly address injustice as an even greater injustice.

However, we must admit that the power of media significantly increases our capacity to instantly and aggressively export victim thinking around the globe. Media does this by dispersing and amplifying biased reports about everyday injustices that would otherwise go mostly unnoticed. Not every injustice should be reported and amplified by mainstream media.

We Decide How to React

Once information is presented to us, each of us has an opportunity to react independently. We must carefully acknowledge our individual responsibility to determine how we react to injustice, instead of allowing the news anchors or gossip columnists to do that for us. Our reaction to personal and public injustice reveals victim thinking. The degree to which any injustice is damaging is not only contingent upon the act itself, but also contingent upon how the recipient of that injustice responds.

"It seems as though our culture is becoming less forgiving, yet more easily offended and more outraged about injustice."

To a person with victim thinking, injustice will most likely be viewed as an insurmountable ordeal. To a person with Zero Victim thinking, that same injustice will be acknowledged as inappropriate and dealt with accordingly, but the impact of the injustice will never be blown out of proportion or used to retaliate against the offender. It will never be used to arouse others to hatred, disrespect, or violence.

The person who committed the injustice will not be demonized, attacked, or canceled. They will be entrusted to the rule of law and offered opportunity for forgiveness and the often-deserved "second chance" if appropriate. The bloody images of people viciously attacked by individuals with victim thinking is reprehensible. Sadly, in many cases the attackers are not arrested or even seen as criminals, but are often hailed as passionate, social justices heroes. If every person in America was severely attacked and demonized for every wrong thing they ever thought, said, or did, none of us could ever hope to recover from our mistakes. As Jesus compassionately spoke of the woman caught in adultery, "He who is without sin among you, let him throw a stone at her first" (John 8:7, NKJV).

Less Forgiving and More Easily Offended: A Toxic Combination

Throughout history, people have thought, said, and done things they shouldn't have. This will certainly continue in the future. It seems as though our culture is becoming less forgiving, yet more easily offended and more outraged about injustice. This strongly suggests the increase of victim mentality in our nation. I believe that people in general are becoming more self-centered in their thinking as spirituality and morality decline. We now commonly think in terms of, "What's best for me." and "What makes me happy." Rarely do we considerately think of others as being as important as ourselves–that their feelings are just as valid as our own. Self-centeredness and victim thinking are a toxic combination.

Put on Some Thicker Skin

Have we ever considered there might be a right way and a wrong way to respond to injustice? Here in America, we can benefit greatly from having "thicker skin" by developing greater mental toughness to deal with offense. We can significantly lessen the impact of injustice by individually developing a Zero Victim Mentality.

A Zero Victim mindset allows you to respond to legitimate victimizations and correct them as necessary, without becoming offended and retaliating against your offender with the intent to cancel or destroy them. Each of us must do our part to insulate our hearts and minds to not allow hurtful words to be hurtful to us. Each of us must ask ourselves, "Do I have an obligation to the greater society to not be deeply offended by the inevitable mistakes of the imperfect people who live within my community?" As my neighbor, you certainly have a responsibility to not offend me. But as your neighbor, I also have a responsibility to you to not be offended by your actions.

Developing a Zero Victim Mentality Requires Skill

As I mentioned previously, we must endeavor to live life from the inside-out and not from the outside-in. We stand a much greater chance of success in life when we work to control what happens within us, instead of what happens to us and what happens around us. You cannot control the rain, but you can decide to carry an umbrella. You cannot stop the flood, but you can decide to build a boat. You may not be able to control the job market, but you can control your personal value and ability to contribute to society as a productive citizen.

The immaturity and ignorance of others that result in offensive words or actions toward you lies beyond your control, but you can regulate your attitude toward them and how you will respond to their unfortunate conduct. Let's explore four techniques that will bring you freedom from offenses and injustice with a Zero Victim Mentality.

1. Develop Humility to Be Able to Pause and Discern

Developing humility begins with several practical steps any person can take to successfully respond to injustice. Here's what humility is not: 1) Humility does not mean thinking less of yourself, but instead means thinking of yourself less. 2) Humility does not undermine your self-worth or diminish your self-esteem. 3) Humility does not require you to willfully subject yourself to disrespect. Humility reminds you that your perception about events, including acts of injustice toward you, does not necessarily reflect the highest level of truth. Therefore, your quick-tempered, instinctive reaction based upon that perception cannot be the ultimate authority in responding to that injustice.

A person who walks in true humility knows that perceptions can be wrong and usually are. Your perception is formulated

"Humility reminds you that your perception about events, including acts of injustice toward you, does not necessarily reflect the highest level of truth."

through information gathered from your senses, which are quite limited. Despite how you feel about an injustice committed against you, you may never know the offender's true motive. I am not at all suggesting that their actions are to be excused or go unchallenged, but you must at least acknowledge that your perceptions about them can be wrong.

The virtue of humility causes an offended individual to pause momentarily, discipline himself or herself to not react emotionally, and then act responsibly by attempting to engage in constructive dialogue with their offender. Humility gives you the best chance of wisely determining the best course of action to be taken in resolving the offense. Thus, a person with a Zero Victim Mentality sees acts of injustice through their Zero Victim lenses with humility.

Imagine what would happen in our nation if every citizen responded to injustice in this manner. Honor and respect would be immediately restored within our society as people responded to offense in a civilized manner. We would once again become a nation of true *ladies* and *gentlemen*, where people related to each other and even their enemies, with dignity and courtesy. I am not referring to a make-believe or utopian society. I am speaking about the tangible, end result of people intentionally cultivating a Zero Victim Mentality by practicing personal humility. This virtue would most certainly help us form a more decent society that ultimately benefits us all.

We seem to forget that our individual well-being is contingent upon the success of our society overall. Selfishness will eventually undermine the health of our society. When people only think and act according to what's best for them, they exalt their personal wishes and preferences above the greater good. I see this as a growing problem in our nation. A country that functions this way is destined to eventually collapse.

In today's culture, taking selfies is the norm. In general, this practice seems to be innocent, so we shouldn't make too much of it. However, I do believe this trend tells us something about ourselves as a nation. At the very least, our infatuation with taking selfies indicates that we celebrate individuals more than families and communities, and is perhaps the beginning stages of a cultural standard of narcissism. I believe this self-centeredness becomes a breeding ground for victim thinking. By reintroducing the virtue of humility in your life, you will safeguard yourself against self-centeredness and victim mentality.

2. Extend Forgiveness to Release You Both

Forgiveness is one of the most important, yet most disregarded practices in community. Any time two imperfect people gather, forgiveness will be necessary in due time. I am frequently disappointed by people's response once offended. More often than not, it seems as though their response to injustice appears punitive as opposed to redemptive. A punitive response aims to punish an offender, whereas a redemptive response seeks to resolve the offense and restore the offender through reconciliation and rehabilitation when possible. I must state that a defiant, unrepentant offender does not deserve restoration. But for the repentant offender, I believe we are morally obligated to extend forgiveness and seek to make amends.

Today, apologies appear irrelevant and no longer acceptable even when they are sincere. In some cases, those offended appear to salivate at the chance to mercilessly destroy the character, reputation, professional image, and career of those who offended them. In doing so, they believe that they are completely justified which is evidence of extreme victim thinking. Conversely, whenever possible, a person with a Zero Victim Mentality seeks occasion to forgive their offender for their actions if at all possible.

When forgiveness is lacking, both the offender and the offended are imprisoned. Victim thinking also occurs when an offended individual becomes a victim of his or her own emotional entrapment. They are not only victim to what their offender did to them, they become captive to the mental bondage of the offense.

Please understand, I am not dismissing the inappropriateness of anything said or done to hurt you. I simply encourage you to ask the question, "Where, when, and how does forgiveness fit into the equation?" Victim thinking explains why the person offended does not extend forgiveness to their offender. We naturally sympathize with the offended and demonize the offender, not realizing that unwillingness to forgive another person can become a secondary injustice.

Forgiveness does not mean forgetting or dismissing the need to execute justice. Let's be honest, you will not likely forget any injustice you've experienced personally. However, Zero Victim Mentality prevents the injustice from controlling your future thoughts, feelings, speech, and behavior, and allows you to extend forgiveness when possible.

3. Cultivate Clear Vision to Keep Looking Ahead

Cultivating clear vision is fundamental to the development of a Zero Victim Mentality. Vision gives you the ability to create

“Vision gives you the ability to create a mental picture of an unrealized future that propels your life forward by decisive action.”

a mental picture of an unrealized future that propels your life forward by decisive action. Without vision, the only picture you'll see is the one created by your past and present realities, which will ultimately define your life. Injustice cannot be futuristic because it has not yet occurred. Contemplating future injustice is an expression of fear and affirms the existence of victim thinking.

Without vision for your future, you will always be limited to focusing on your immediate challenges and rehearsing past events. Victim thinkers often think and speak about injustices committed against them in the past and complain about things not being what they should be in the present. On the contrary, Zero Victim thinkers characteristically believe that neither past nor present events are capable of hindering them from being successful in the future. They are fearless!

Cultivating clear vision aids in the development of a Zero Victim Mentality by resizing offenses–making them smaller–and thus reducing the magnitude of their effect on your life. For the individual who possesses a clear and grand vision, offenses matter little as they see the bigger picture. Their offenses are literally swallowed up by their future outlook and future opportunities.

Dr. Martin Luther King Jr. serves as our greatest recent example of the power of vision operating in the life of an individual who demonstrated Zero Victim thinking. Known for his *I Have a Dream* speech and nonviolent protest throughout the Civil Rights Movement, Dr. King suffered persecution, imprisonment, and ultimately assassination. I believe that his nonviolent response to the numerous and grave injustices he experienced was connected to his vision. Dr. King possessed a clear mental picture of the future of our nation, which propelled him forward by decisive action, and empowered him with the discipline needed

"Cultivating clear vision aids in the development of a Zero Victim Mentality by resizing offenses—making them smaller—and thus reducing the magnitude of their effect on your life."

to not retaliate against his offenders. His vision allowed him to put the injustices he suffered in the right context.

Evidenced by his dream and refusal to embrace the victim role, I have concluded that Dr. King did indeed possess a Zero Victim Mentality. In light of your current vision for your life, think about your own past or present offenses. Are they really as big as they seem? Was as much damage done as you think there was? Is that damage permanent and irreversible? Do you consider the relationship between you and the person who offended you irreconcilable? Are you strong enough to extend forgiveness toward your offender?

I would encourage you to not allow past or present offenses to define your life. Resize those offenses within the context of your larger future vision, remembering you have limited time and energy to accomplish it. As you deliberately implement this principle of Zero Victim thinking, I believe your negative sentiments about any offenses in life will gradually fade.

4. Affirm Your Identity: You Are Not a Victim!

The last principle you can employ as you develop a Zero Victim mindset is to affirm your identity. Absolutely knowing that you are not a victim is the surest way to avoid victim mentality. In my twenty one years of marriage, I have never struggled to decide which of my wife's dresses I should wear or which color lipstick I should put on because I am a man! This is true not because I *feel* like a man, but because I *know* that God created me to be a man. My behavior as a man reflects what I know and believe to be true about my identity as a man.

Questioning our identity or struggling with identity crisis welcomes victim mentality. King Solomon comments, "For as he [a man] thinks in his heart, so is he" (Proverbs 23:7, NKJV). If you believe in your heart that you are a victim, your thoughts, speech, and behavior will all serve to affirm your identity as a victim. You will live out the characteristics of a victim because you have assumed the identity of a victim. Even if others attempt to convince you that you are not a victim, your assessment of your own identity will overrule their positive opinion.

Zero Victim thinking results from knowing exactly who you are. Even when presented with an occasion to feel like a victim or play the victim role, your identity will displace your feelings, reminding you that you are not a victim and therefore must not behave like one. As you develop a Zero Victim mindset, your identity as a non-victim will be solidified and affirmed. Nothing and no one will ever again cause you to believe you are a victim. Even if the most unfortunate injustice is committed against you, whether discrimination, racism, or slander, you will always see through your Zero Victim lenses, confirming your identity as a non-victim.

These four techniques will help to properly equip you to receive any injustice that comes your way. To revisit our baseball analogy, once prepared, the possibility of you being injured by that fastball of injustice will be significantly reduced and even eliminated. As injustices and offenses come–and they will come–they will simply be caught and stopped.

CHAPTER ELEVEN

Hear No Victim, See No Victim, Be No Victim!

To move from victim mentality to Zero Victim Mentality, we must carefully consider the role our words play in shaping our lives. The words we consistently hear and speak greatly impact our conscious and subconscious minds. Whether positive or negative, if we hear the same message enough, we will eventually begin to believe what we hear. This is especially true for children. Over time, we become a self-fulfilling prophecy of the words we speak.

Victim mentality can often be traced back to an individual's childhood, just as my personal journey toward a Zero Victim Mentality began there. Studies show that humans are mentally most vulnerable and most easily influenced during the developmental years of their childhood. A government adviser, Frank Field, claimed that wealthier children from stable homes hear 440,000 more positive comments from their parents than children from dysfunctional families by the age of three.[6] Field claims that the level of communication between a parent and child proves a greater impact on a child's future than socio-economic class or ethnicity.

We must carefully consider the wisdom of King Solomon, once thought to be the wisest man who ever lived. In one of his proverbs he comments, "Death and life are in the power of the tongue, and those who love it will eat its fruit" (Proverbs 18:21, NKJV). Field's research supports the ancient wisdom of King Solomon in reminding us of the power of words spoken and unspoken.

Victim mentality is often a direct result of words communicated or not communicated to an individual. People of influence and authority such as parents, pastors, teachers, coaches, and corporate leaders, can cause extensive damage to an individual's mentality by speaking destructive words over them. Equally, the silence or failure to speak words of life can also be damaging.

Words Have Pervasive Power

You may not be aware of this, but the probability is high that you or someone you know has been a victim of verbal abuse. Although there are different types of abuse, verbal abuse is most common and easily becomes a liability for everyone who possesses the ability to communicate. Verbal abuse happens intentionally and unintentionally at home, at work, or at school. This abuse

[6] "Middle-class children 'hear 23MILLION more words than poorer children before they start school,' " Mail Online, http://www.dailymail.co.uk/news/article-2140306/Middle-class-children-hear-23MILLION-words-poorer-children-start-school.html.

> "To move from victim mentality to Zero Victim Mentality, we must carefully consider the role our words play in shaping our lives."

can originate with people we know and love, or with complete strangers. Verbal abuse encompasses teasing, demeaning, trivializing, name-calling, and scolding. Because of the moral depravity of the human heart and the vast scope of verbal abuse, this abuse cannot be prevented or completely stopped.

Verbal abuse can be difficult to detect because its effects are not physically seen, and therefore cannot be easily identified. Victims of verbal abuse sometimes live for many years or even their entire life, without knowing they have been abused. This hidden abuse becomes perpetually damaging simply because you cannot solve a problem that you don't know exists. To neutralize the damaging effects of verbal abuse, the victim must first identify the abuse, and then pursue deliberate and strategic intervention to end the cycle of victimization.

Thousands of people are victimized through verbal abuse every day. Without specific intervention, the effects of negative words will usually last a lifetime. Words carry meaning and inherently possess the power to define. Because individuals are defined by words, their identity forms as a result. In time, people literally become the words spoken over them.

This practice can be tragic when dealing with children. Imagine what happens mentally and emotionally to a child searching for their identity, purpose, and value, when they constantly hear abusive phrases such as, "You are so stupid!" "You can't do anything right!" or "I wish you were never born!" As the father of two wonderful and very bright children, the thought of this tragedy sickens me and breaks my heart.

Unfortunately, this reality exists for millions of children each day. These children become severely damaged mentally and emotionally, and damaged children soon become damaged adults, who usually damage other people. As a pastor, I have observed how hurt people hurt people, and how victims make victims. Pain becomes their norm. Damaged adults with victim mentalities, will most likely repeat the cycle of injury by becoming verbally abusive parents to their own children.

Verbal Abuse Creates Victim Mentality

The far-reaching effects of verbal abuse are impossible to quantify. Victims of verbal abuse often struggle with low self-esteem, low self-worth, and even self-hatred. Within their minds, they easily compare and contrast themselves to other people, oftentimes believing themselves to be inferior.

As they further embrace negative words spoken about them, the stage is set for a life plagued by victim mentality. Their future is now likely to be characterized by a negative outlook of life that stems from an unhealthy self-image. They can only relate to others out of their own personal pain. In some cases, violence, rebellion, drug addiction, and sexual immorality become likely consequences.

The high probability of being a recipient of verbal abuse makes positive, mental conditioning and preconditioning critically important for each of us. The development of a Zero Victim Mentality can be used to effectively accomplish three goals in life: 1) To neutralize the unfavorable effects of verbal abuse; 2) To begin the process of restoring a healthy and positive self-image; and 3) To change your future outlook from being pessimistic to optimistic. A Zero Victim mindset will move you from a life of fear to a life of faith.

Life Lenses: What Do You See?

If you've ever worn eyeglasses or sunglasses, you know what it means to look through a set of lenses. The prescription and tint of those lenses affect everything you see through them. For a person in need of prescription eyeglasses, good vision isn't possible without the right set of lenses. Without them, their vision becomes obscured, which causes things to appear to be something different than what they really are.

Lenses are intended to adjust vision on an individual basis. All prescriptions are personal. In most cases, eyeglasses are custom-fitted with an exclusive prescription for the wearer. Two people who need eyeglasses cannot simply switch glasses. Each of them needs the pair of glasses created just for them. Based upon the lenses they are looking through, two different people can observe the same object, but see very different images.

People wearing sunglasses also see differently. Imagine one person wearing sunglasses with black tint and another person wearing sunglasses with brown tint. If both people observe a white vehicle passing by, the vehicle would somewhat appear to be light gray to one and light brown to the other, even though the actual color of the vehicle is white.

It would be ridiculous for a person wearing sunglasses to walk outside on a sunny day and complain about the sun being dim. In each of these examples, the lenses the person is wearing at a particular moment in time affects their perception about reality.

Victim Lenses Ruin Lives

For each of us, our mentality represents our personal set of lenses through which we see and filter everything in life. Our

"Our mentality represents
our personal set of lenses
through which we see and
filter everything in life."

experiences and conversations and interpretations of them are tinted by the "color" of our mental lenses. What you see through your lenses defines "your world." Despite what circumstances and events really are in the actual world, they will always appear to be something different in "your world," which creates a different, privatized reality just for you. I believe this powerful concept explains why our nation is becoming more divided racially and politically. Many people are embracing victim mentality and seeing life through their private set of victim lenses.

Victim lenses are very expensive! They cause individuals to perceive unfortunate events that happen to them as a potential threat or attack against them, even when they may not be. In every conversation, they wonder if something negative is being said about them or if they are being criticized in some way. These people tend to perceive themselves as the recipient of ill will or as the object of some form of personal attack. It is usually necessary to approach them with great caution because they are so easily offended. Similar to reading glasses, they "read" victimization into everything they see or experience. Even when other people are not directly referring to them, a person who sees through victim lenses perceives that they are being talked about negatively or attacked.

This false perception causes victims to live fearful and stressful lives. They sometimes suffer unnecessary panic attacks. Imagine living in a perpetual state of anticipation of a calamity that never comes. This thinking makes it nearly impossible to enjoy life. As a result, relationships with your spouse, family, and friends are adversely affected.

Victim lenses can also serve to create a self-defeatist attitude. Self-criticism is common among those with a high degree of victim thinking. They can often be heard making statements like, "I am such a loser!" "I am so stupid!" or "Good things never happen to me!" Whenever I hear people make such comments, I consider their words to be proof that they are struggling with victim thinking.

People only speak negatively about themselves because they see themselves through victim lenses. This mentality can be accompanied by attitudes and perceptions of hopelessness, pessimism, and failure. In many cases, even when a person with a victim mentality is encouraged, they cannot receive the encouragement as being valid. A person wearing victim lenses perceives that they will lose regardless of what happens or what anyone else says to the contrary.

Rising Above with Zero Victim Lenses

Now imagine what would happen if you possessed a pair of lenses that magically caused you to see every day as a sunny day, even while heavy rain or snow was falling outside. Some would reject this idea as being silly and absurd. Others would conclude those lenses were deceptive and presented a false sense of reality.

On the contrary, I believe these lenses would not be deceptive at all, but would actually present a more accurate representation of what is factually true. Although not visible from a surface level on earth, scientifically speaking, every day is indeed a sunny day above the clouds. Really, since the beginning of time, there has never been a cloudy day. If you've ever flown in an airplane on a rainy day, you have witnessed this truth ten to fifteen minutes into your flight. Beneath the clouds, everything is dark. But once you pass through the clouds, it seems as though you've entered into a different world altogether.

Just as victim lenses cause individuals to perceive themselves and their circumstances from the perspective of a victim, Zero Victim lenses will empower you to know that you are not a victim. With a Zero Victim Mentality, you will always be able to see beyond the clouds and "your world" will always be bright. Instead of seeing yourself as a victim of something undesirable, you will always see yourself as the ultimate winner, which then defines your very identity. The more you "see" winning, the more you will believe you are a winner, and victory will eventually become your only reality.

You Can't Lose with Zero Victim Lenses!

As you develop a Zero Victim Mentality, you will gradually eliminate the possibility of ever perceiving yourself as a victim. You will discover that it literally becomes difficult to be offended by other people. I have become such a Zero Victim thinker, I find it almost impossible to identify problems. Imagine the frustration you will cause those who intend to offend you! You will minimize the chances of erroneously perceiving people or circumstances as forces against you. Even when they are, you will be better equipped to act and not react in those situations, and not be controlled or manipulated by them. Your interpretation of those events will not affect your attitude or overall perception about yourself or your life. By wearing Zero Victim lenses, you insulate yourself against victimization, and strip others of their power to control or manipulate your emotions.

"By wearing Zero Victim lenses, you insulate yourself against victimization, and strip others of their power to control or manipulate your emotions."

Just as a person with victim lenses will tend to "read" victimization into circumstances, a person with Zero Victim lenses will tend to "read" victimization out of circumstances. When you hear other people insulting you, you will automatically conclude that this must be a case of mistaken identity, because the person they are describing is definitely not you. I believe this principle can really help our nation diffuse the growing racial tension we're presently experiencing. Instead of having a self-defeatist perception of yourself, you will begin to rightfully celebrate yourself with humility. You will start to define your life based upon who and what you are, instead of who and what others say you are not.

Your Zero Victim lenses will cause fear and stress to decrease significantly in your life. You will ultimately experience increased productivity and perform at higher levels of excellence because your thinking is no longer clouded by thoughts and emotions that stem from victimization.

This new attitude of winning will project hope, optimism, confidence, and courage in all you do. The overall quality of your life will improve, enabling you to better enjoy your life. Your relationships will deepen and become more passionate. These are just a few of the many benefits of liberating yourself from the mentality of defeat, and rising above injustice with a new attitude by putting on Zero Victim lenses. Once you put these lenses on, never take them off! And for the remainder of your life, no matter what happens to you or around you, you will see yourself winning in life.

“Your Zero Victim lenses will cause fear and stress to decrease significantly in your life.”

Victim Talk Versus Zero Victim Talk

Whenever we need to describe an object, we do so based upon what we perceive it to be through our senses, primarily our sight. What you see through your mental lenses will eventually be reflected in the way you talk. All of us tend to say what we see and think. Jesus made a profound observation that speaks to this idea:

> *Brood of vipers! How can you, being evil, speak good things? For out of the abundance of the heart the mouth speaks. A good man out of the good treasure of his heart brings forth good things, and an evil man out of the evil treasure brings forth evil things* (Matthew 12:34-35, NKJV).

While lecturing a group of religious leaders about hypocrisy, Jesus enlightens them about the origin of the words they were speaking. He explained how it is impossible for a person to speak something different than what they really believe in their hearts. What you carry in your heart will eventually be spoken out of your mouth.

A person with a victim mentality will speak victim language. When they speak, victim talk is spoken by reflex in response to their circumstances in life. On the contrary, a person with a Zero Victim mindset will speak Zero Victim language by reflex. As Jesus stated, a good man out of the good treasure of his heart brings forth good things.

Here are five common examples of victim talk compared to Zero Victim talk:

VICTIM STATEMENT	ZERO VICTIM STATEMENT
"You owe me an apology!"	"People are flawed and we all make mistakes."
"I'll show them!"	"I won't let that bother me because I'm confident in who I am."
"Why are you always so mean to me?"	"Is there something that I'm doing that bothers you? If so, let's discuss it."
"I feel like such a loser."	"I see myself winning in everything I do!"
"This is all your fault!"	"How can we do things differently in the future?"

These victim statements are quite common in our normal conversations. If these victim statements are routinely spoken out of your mouth, I want to encourage you to practice replacing them with the Zero Victim statements. By doing so, you will train your mind to better respond to the daily pitfalls of victimization. You will also train your tongue to answer in a more gracious manner. Remember, a Zero Victim thinker always acts and never reacts.

The primary difference between the two statement categories is simple–the victim statements are based upon emotional feelings from a self-centered perspective, while the Zero Victim statements are based upon decisive thoughts from a greater perspective. You will also notice that most of the victim statements tend to pass responsibility. Each of them imply that someone else should be blamed or held responsible for the victim's perceived misfortune.

Each Zero Victim statement initially accepts personal responsibility and assigns blame to no one. An individual with a Zero Victim Mentality always seeks to intentionally act, and never carelessly reacts out of emotional frustration. They have been empowered to positively respond, because their identity as a non-victim has been affirmed and solidified. They have conditioned their mind to see incidents through their Zero Victim lenses.

We must be mentally prepared for the moments when victimization is presented to us. Our response is always a choice and not just a feeling. The decision to be a victim or not be a victim happens in a split second, and is immediately evidenced by your words. For most of us, we say what we feel before we even think. We respond by reflex, which confirms just how critical preconditioning our mind is to avoid victim thinking. A spontaneous and emotional, *feel good* reaction requires far less energy and effort than a contemplative, intentional, and disciplined response. This latter kind of reaction will always be seen and heard from individuals who have successfully developed a Zero Victim Mentality.

Political Correctness Is a Flawed Idea

Political correctness has spawned from victim thinking in America. Merriam-Webster defines politically correct as *conforming to a belief that language and practices which could offend political sensibilities (as in matters of sex or race) should be eliminated.*[7] If you look at this particular definition closely, it suggests that a person's speech and behavior should be eliminated

---

[7] Merriam-Webster, http://www.merriam-webster.com/dictionary/politically%20 correct.

“An individual with a Zero Victim Mentality always seeks to intentionally act, and never carelessly reacts out of emotional frustration.”

because of the *potential* to offend, even when the offense has not happened and may not even occur. This presents an impossible challenge for anyone. How can we possibly modify our words and conduct in advance to prevent an unrealized possibility from happening? To do so, we would need to be mind readers.

Political correctness attempts to govern an individual's speech, attitude, and conduct based upon a *potential perceived* injustice. This is a twice-flawed idea, because *potential perception* is unsubstantiated and completely subjective. Political correctness anticipates victimization and labels everyone a victim, even before a legitimate offense has occurred. This is prejudiced thinking! This ideal can be seen in existence in government, in media, in corporations, and on university campuses. This illegitimate ideology has overtaken our society and paved the way for *cancel culture*.

I believe political correctness explicitly contributes to the progression of victim thinking for two major reasons. First, the idea is based entirely upon subjective belief and perception, which are both internal realities. If an individual believes something to be true and perceives people and events in a particular manner, no one is capable of changing their belief and perception.

No matter how much evidence is presented or how well you defend your position in a debate, you cannot change the way another person has dogmatically decided to think or feel. In this case, the issue is not what they think, but how they think. The hate-filled interactions we see between people today is not because people are thinking different things. It's usually because they are thinking differently about the same things. Some people see through victim lenses while others do not.

"Political correctness attempts to govern an individual's speech, attitude, and conduct based upon a *potential perceived* injustice."

None of us can alter another person's mind where their beliefs and perceptions are formulated. When beliefs and perceptions are accurate and positive, your mind is fixed with unshakeable convictions that will impact your circumstances for the better. However, when your beliefs and perceptions are inaccurate and negative, you cannot be easily swayed toward right thinking and your circumstances will tend to become worse.

Our beliefs and perceptions are often communicated as feelings, which tend to change like the weather forecast. A person with a victim mentality can experience similar events and feel differently about each of them. As a result, your interaction with them will be characterized by inconsistencies and unpredictable interactions.

Personal feelings are very strong and are very influential in our lives. Let's be honest. Each of us tend to prejudge how we feel about people, and whether or not we like or dislike them, based upon limited interaction with them or understanding about them. The result of attempting to manage these abstract feelings with political correctness feels chaotic at best.

The second problem with political correctness is that it caters to an individual's capacity to be offended and anticipates them being offended, even when they actually may not be. Political correctness works as a blanket rule concerning offense that applies to everyone. Its application is random and defective for the simple fact that no two people will respond to a potentially offensive incident in the same way. What offends one individual may not offend another at all. While political correctness in some instances may possibly benefit an easily offended person, at the same time it censors the words and behavior of everyone else–a clear instance of discrimination against them.

"Our beliefs and perceptions are often communicated as feelings, which tend to change like the weather forecast."

Political correctness is a concealed, fear-based method of controlling people that complements and perpetuates victim mentality. Political correctness changes freedom of speech into freedom to limit speech. Tyrannical in nature, political correctness suppresses an individual's freedom to share unconventional thoughts and creative ideas, while claiming to protect individuals who possess a victim mentality. Every organization needs the cross exchange of thoughts and ideas (even if they are offensive) in order to move forward. Therefore, political correctness slows growth and innovation. I'm certainly not endorsing offensive or hate-filled speech, but a person's potential perception about what you may say should not be used to deny you the right to speak.

The Importance of Community-Wide Zero Victim Mentality

As any community grows, it becomes more diverse in terms of the beliefs, perceptions, and ideologies represented within that community. This increases the probability of conflicting points of view. In every sizable group, the cultivation of Zero Victim thinking will prove to be beneficial.

No two people will ever see everything eye to eye and completely agree on all things. In my many years of organizational leadership, I have discovered only one way to stop offenses. You cannot stop people from offending others, but you can stop individuals from being offended, if they develop a Zero Victim mindset. I believe our endeavors to stop offenses by attempting to establish a politically correct society are futile.

"Political correctness
changes freedom of speech
into freedom to limit speech."

Victim Mentality Spread by People of Influence

After enough conversations with enough people, you'd quickly find that victims are scattered throughout every segment of society. People with victim mentalities are not easily identified and appear to be normal, everyday people. Because of this we must ask the question, "How does victim mentality affect our culture on a larger scale?" Individuals as well as people groups can be hampered by victim mentality. Within organizations, victim thinking can also become a culture.

In assessing qualities for leadership positions and job opportunities, employers tend to primarily look for and value academic and experiential qualifications. You rarely hear about a job interview in which a candidate was carefully questioned about their emotional qualification to perform the job successfully. I have discovered that a leader can be highly educated while also possessing a high degree of victim mentality.

The challenge of having leaders beset with victim thinking in positions of influence, is that hurt people tend to hurt people and victims make victims. Perhaps you've heard the adage *one bad apple will spoil the bunch*. Organizationally speaking, I would argue that *one bad apple* will absolutely *spoil the bunch*, especially when the *apple* holds a position of leadership or influence. Their rotten, victim thinking will affect the entire organization. The strengths and weaknesses of any leader will inevitably affect the culture of the organization they lead.

A CEO with a victim mentality will see their company through victim lenses and will make decisions influenced by their victim thinking. Their *victim leadership* will ultimately affect the employees and customers of their company. An elected government official with a victim mentality will tend to create and implement *victim policies* that affect the citizens they represent, and possibly the entire community or nation.

A schoolteacher with a victim mentality will teach *victim lessons* to the students in their classroom. Even pastors with a victim mentality will preach *victim sermons* to their congregations based upon *victim theology*. From these examples, you can clearly see the importance of assessing the existence of victim thinking before appointing people to positions of leadership.

CHAPTER TWELVE

The Effects and Affects of Living in a Hostile World

Several years ago, I drove from my home in Chicago to my parents' home in Tuscaloosa, Alabama. While driving south on I-65, a state trooper in Kentucky stopped me for speeding. I was indeed driving above the speed limit when I passed his parked car, and I immediately knew I was in trouble when he turned his lights on. I received a citation for exceeding the posted speed limit. Being stopped by the police officer was not an injustice. I was wrong. But because of this unfortunate event, my mind took a mental picture of the scenery around me. To this very day, that location is a place I cannot forget.

Even though I didn't know my exact location when I received the citation, each time I drive along that route, I recognize the place where the officer stopped me. As a result, I instinctively reduce my speed and drive more cautiously. I always comment to my wife, "This is where I got that speeding ticket!" Because something undesirable happened to me there, each time I'm in that same spot, I mentally re-live that traumatic moment and my behavior is consciously and subconsciously affected.

Similar to my experience with the speeding ticket, negative events permanently impact us at conscious and subconscious levels. Even when we try to forget those experiences, we usually cannot. Whenever we encounter similar conditions, they often stimulate some kind of reaction within us.

Neuroscience explains how the brain records and stores every detail of every event in life. Even when we cannot readily recall specific events, our brains never forget them. When we find ourselves in a potential hostile setting reminiscent of a previous unpleasant experience, our minds automatically identify the threat of being victimized once again. The thought comes to us either consciously or subconsciously, "I remember what happened the last time." We instinctively heighten our awareness of possible injury and choose to proceed with caution and even suspicion. We automatically react by *reducing our speed*, just as I still do when driving through Kentucky many years later.

Our unfortunate experiences in life produce negative effects and affects. None of us is immune or insulated from injustice and painful experiences. Therefore, we must understand the difference between effects and affects in order to avoid victim mentality and adequately deal with it when it comes.

In general, think of an effect as being tangible, whereas an affect is intangible. An effect is associated with a cause, but an affect relates to a response to a cause. For example, the *effect* of

"Negative events permanently impact us at conscious and subconscious levels."

me disrespecting you would certainly *affect* our relationship. As an effect, injustice is a stimulus that causes us to think and feel a certain way. As an affect, injustice produces a response that determines how we think and feel, and ultimately alters our future behavior.

Victim Mentality Comes from Past Experiences

Victim mentality has an upside. Whenever we perceive hostilities, our minds react by taking the defensive posture necessary to deal with legitimate threats. Conversely, on occasions where legitimate threats do not exist, victim mentality becomes a mental liability by producing the affects of unwarranted fear and suspicion of others, while impacting our associations with them.

This can often be observed in our relationships. Individuals who have experienced failed relationships in the past often struggle mentally when entering new relationships. In some cases, they are prone to anticipate the failure of a new relationship because of failure in the past. Past circumstances are sometimes interpreted in a way that allows people to *see* problems, even when problems aren't there. Likewise, when faced with repeated rejection, individuals often develop a tendency to lose confidence because of anticipated failure. Whether interviewing for a job or submitting a college application, whether rich or poor, the affect of victim thinking can shake a person's confidence because of the past effect of a negative experience.

The Rich Victim—Yes, There Is Such a Thing!

As a child, George Gaston journeyed to the United States of America as the only son of immigrant parents who endured the Great Depression. Well into his adult years, George could not forget the awful conditions of extreme poverty his family faced during his childhood. As a child, he was too familiar with every homeless shelter and soup kitchen in town. On countless nights, George went to bed hungry, angry at the world, and angry with his parents. In his anger, he solemnly vowed he would find a way to make as much money as he possibly could–however he could–to avoid re-living the horrible memories of his dreadful childhood.

By age sixteen, George had become a skilled and efficient worker who could repair almost anything. Good with his hands, he possessed a tremendous work ethic. He started a small business doing home repairs, but it didn't take long for word about George to spread all over town. He quickly found himself with more work than he could handle, so he hired a few other men and began renovating properties.

Having grown up in poverty, George knew the value of saving money and managing money wisely. He used the profits he made from his renovation business to buy foreclosed apartment buildings, refurbish them, and sell them to investors with high profit margins. As his business rapidly grew, George dealt with numerous lawsuits regarding questionable business practices. In less than ten years, George became a multi-millionaire and one of the richest and most powerful men in his town.

During an interview, a local reporter questioned George. "Mr. Gaston, you are known for your ability to overcome all odds and succeed. You seem to always win. What bit of advice would you give to a child who one day wants to be as successful as you are?" Remembering the bitterness of his poverty-ridden childhood and the promise he made to himself, George replied, "You must get 'yours' however you can because no one will help you, and no one can be trusted!"

George now used his money, status, and power to fulfill the oath he swore to himself as a child. He concluded that as long as he controlled his life, the world around him, and the people around him, no one could ever take advantage of him. George intended to use his money and power as weapons to protect himself. He determined he would never again experience lack, go to bed hungry, or be without a home.

Even as a successful entrepreneur, George developed a victim mentality as the result of his unfortunate experiences as a child. His success, money, and influence served to camouflage and empower his victim thinking. In George's case, we see that success and wealth sometimes conceal victim thinking. George did not make money to help others. He made money to insulate himself against the pain he experienced as a child. The effect of poverty greatly affected George's character and motives in business.

In a society where money answers all things, financial success is desired and preferred by every citizen. But how many people like George are motivated to amass financial resources and power, only to protect themselves from being victims? How many of them have sacrificed their integrity by engaging in unethical practices because of their fear of failing to meet the expectations of others? Although acquiring money is capable of preventing hardship for our families, doing so with motives that stem from a victim mentality bears great consequences.

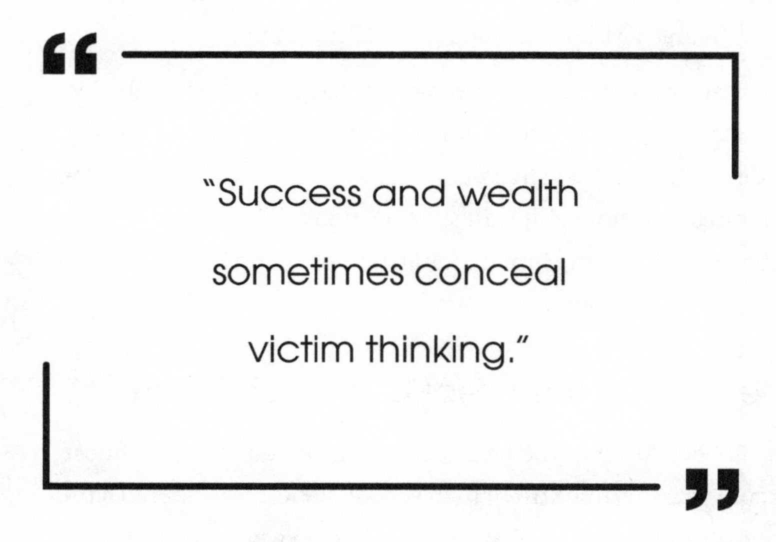
"Success and wealth
sometimes conceal
victim thinking."

George's victim mentality caused him to prosper financially, but in the process of doing so he completely lost compassion for people. George was financially prosperous, but relationally poor. His quest to avoid the pain associated with financial lack caused him to become cold and insensitive toward others. He viewed people only as objects to be used in helping him succeed. The effect of victim thinking affected George by resulting in three failed marriages. In each marriage, George's love for money proved to be greater than his love for his wife. Victim thinking made George a rich man, but not a wealthy man.

If not stewarded correctly, money easily becomes a shell for victims to withdraw into to protect them from perceived danger. In George's case, that shell became a barrier separating him from meaningful relationships. Despite his financial success, which he believed would bring him freedom, George found himself captive as a mental prisoner of victim mentality.

The Poor Victim Affect Isn't Much Different

Robert Rosen worked for Pacific-Central Railroad for almost twenty years. While still in high school, Robert was offered a full time job and decided to drop out of school to work. Robert was never interested in completing or furthering his education by taking advantage of the tuition reimbursement program offered by Pacific-Central. What Robert lacked in formal education, he made up for in efficiency, dependability, and hard work on the job.

At seventeen, Robert fathered his first child by the woman he was dating at the time. By thirty-seven, though never married, Robert had fathered four children and was expecting another with his girlfriend. One day Robert was called into his foreman's office.

"Robert, you've been with us for many years, and you know how much I appreciate you. You are one of my best workers. I hate to tell you this, but corporate made some changes in the way we do things here. They've decided to automate our switching systems to reduce overhead expenses, which means your current job is being eliminated immediately. Three new positions are available in our department, but they require a high school diploma and at least two years of college education, which you don't have. Robert, I'm really sorry, but I have to let you go."

"Let me go? But...but this is the only job I've ever had. I barely make enough money now to feed my family. What about them? What am I supposed to do? This just isn't fair! I've worked all these years for this company and now I'm losing my job? Those rich guys at corporate don't care about people like me. They wear their fancy suits and play golf several times a week, while the rest of us do all the hard work! If they cared about people like me, they wouldn't take away our jobs. They would take less money and give more to the people who need it like me."

Six years later, Robert was still unemployed. Several job offers were presented to him, but each required a high school diploma and a skillset to work with spreadsheets and inventory software. Robert barely survived by relying on government assistance and support from local charities. He believed whatever he could get from these agencies was the least they could do for people like him–people made victims at the hands of those he believed were greedy. Still today, Robert strongly feels entitled to receive support from the government and various agencies because he cannot find another job that accommodates him as well as Pacific-Central once did.

Robert developed a victim mentality. Unfortunately, he failed to honestly admit his negligence in making wise decisions earlier in life. We often fail to realize the impact our decisions will have on our future. Robert would not take responsibility for his decisions to start a family in high school and discontinue his high school education. His failure to continue his education caused him to be unprepared for the developing job market and ultimately disqualified him for the technological changes at Pacific-Central.

Frustrated by his past experiences, Robert believes all corporate executives are selfish and greedy. He believes our capitalistic way of doing business is corrupt and unfair, and that our nation is desperately in need of a government that favors socialism. Robert chooses to disregard the role of corporate executives in employing several thousands of people, allowing them to provide comfortable lifestyles for their families and live as tax paying citizens. Robert developed a victim mentality and believed he deserved financial assistance because of the economic injustice he unfairly suffered at the hands of others.

The Affect of the Perception Effect

Both George and Robert developed a victim mentality as a result of their perception about their circumstances. Although their experiences are considerably different, their mentalities are the same. George's success and Robert's lack of success were both fueled by past perceptions of injustice. Victim mentality affects people on every socio-economic level.

Even when a legitimate threat does not exist, even the perception of a threat stimulates victim mentality, causing individuals to live defensively. Anytime we develop a perception

"We often fail to realize the impact our decisions will have on our future."

about something, we draw conclusions based upon our finite senses and limited personal interpretation of events. The problem with perceptions is the high probability our perceptions can be wrong. Apart from events and circumstances, perceptions are developed within the mind where victim mentality resides. Whether an actual injustice was or was not committed, victimization always begins as a perception within the mind. When a perceived threat is valid, self-defense can be appropriate and necessary. However, when a perceived threat is invalid, victim mentality usually results in harm being done to ourselves and to other people.

One of my mentors, Dr. Robb Thompson, often says that a person we love can do no wrong and a person we hate can do no right. This quote articulates the power of perception. When we perceive that we like an individual, we tend to overlook their inappropriate behavior. When we perceive that we don't like a person, we tend to overlook their good intentions. Wrong perceptions result in victim mentality for us, but also create wrong perceptions about those we have no relationship with. Victim thinking is prejudiced thinking, because it causes an individual to draw conclusions about people they don't know and events that have not transpired.

Real Victims Suffer Because of Victim Thinking

In a growing culture of subjective reasoning with personal interpretations of morality, blame, and accusation, we must carefully delineate the difference between real acts of victimization and pervasive victim thinking. Victim mentality must be identified and called out, because victim thinking often

"The problem with perceptions is the high probability our perceptions can be wrong."

causes real victims of injustice to suffer. Victim thinkers often represent the proverbial boy who cried wolf.

Just a few years ago, our nation endured the elongated congressional hearing of Dr. Christine Blasey Ford's accusation of then Judge Brett Kavanaugh. When the hearing ended, I was deeply saddened to see that an unproven accusation of sexual misconduct garnered more attention and government resources than the millions of proven acts of sexual misconduct and opens cases of sex trafficking. I am in no position to declare Dr. Ford or now Justice Kavanaugh innocent or guilty. But I do believe the highly publicized circus witnessed by the American people and people around the world, to some extent dishonored the many true victims of sexual misconduct.

Just imagine if their legitimate cases had received the same level of scrutiny and outcry. What if the millions of dollars of time invested, legal fees, media coverage, and government resources were utilized to help true victims? Justice Kavanaugh's family suffered, as well as all men of integrity who must now consider if their character can also be so easily tarnished or their innocent actions misconstrued. I denounce any inappropriate conduct by a man toward a woman. But this case proved that accusation is easily weaponized. Concerning the Ford-Kavanaugh hearing, I believe there were no winners.

I sincerely believe that our law enforcement agencies should and must do all they can to prosecute those who victimize innocent people to the fullest extent of our law. But I also believe that the irresponsible and trivial actions of victim thinkers who victimize innocent people should also be considered criminal. We cannot allow an individual's effort to live a life of character and moral integrity to be so easily dismantled with unsubstantiated claims.

It should not be that people with unchecked and unquestioned emotional reactions, are so easily capable of bringing unmerited and unproven accusations against innocent people, to slander against their character and damage their families without consequence. These actions are violently criminal! More and more, we're seeing people coalescing and gathering around their perceived common pains and victimizations, and weaponizing their perceived injustices to attack and condemn innocent people or those that disagree with them on socio-political issues.

Morals and Values Go M.I.A.

Living in a hostile world contributes significantly to the shaping of our personal morals and values, which collectively become our national morals and values. Unfortunately, morality seems to be rapidly declining in the United States and around the world. As I mentioned before, victim thinking causes us to live from a defensive posture because we feel the need to protect ourselves from a perceived threat. When we conclude other people and institutions are against us, we tend to live self-centered lives where we become primarily and blindly concerned about *our* needs and doing what pleases *us*. Because we don't expect our enemies to care for us, self-preservation and self-interest become our number one focus. We seek to avoid victimization at all costs, eventually producing an entire society characterized by cultural victim thinking. We live our lives caring mostly for ourselves and not for other people.

I propose that this self-centered, self-serving victim thinking, multiplied in the lives of millions of citizens within a nation, serves as a catalyst to national moral decline. Victim thinking encourages people to become less considerate, less kind, and less tolerant of others. I believe that the significant increase in the number of abortions and the widespread acceptance of the practice is a clear expression of nationalized victim mentality. Abortion statistics vividly portray this truth. It is not my intent to address this issue politically, but morally in light of the effect and affect of victim thinking.

According to the Guttmacher Institute, from 1973 through 2011, nearly 53 million legal abortions occurred in the U.S.[8] This appalling number does not include the number of illegal abortions. Regardless of our various political positions regarding the subject of abortion, the elimination of 53 million citizens for any reason is an unthinkable calamity of epic proportions.

What does this tragic statistic really say about our nation? In my assessment, among other conclusions that can be drawn, the statistic affirms widespread victim mentality and how victim thinking has impacted our overall morals and values as a nation. Victim mentality always encourages a self-centered, self-serving focus and inhibits the consideration of what's best for others. Concerning this horrific number of abortions, in most cases mothers with victim mentalities made decisions in their own interests, not considering the interests of their unborn children. These women had their "right" to be victims protected through supporting legislation that caters to victim mentality. Anytime a woman simply feels that she has been victimized, she

[8] "U.S. Abortion Statistics," Abort73.com, http://www.abort73.com/abortion_facts/us_abortion_statistics/.

"Victim thinking encourages people to become less considerate, less kind, and less tolerant of others."

can conveniently decide to terminate life in her womb. Victim thinking has indeed contributed to the astronomical number of abortions conducted in our nation.

Immoral Citizens Run Amok in a Victim Mentality Nation

A notable characteristic of the individuals in a moral nation is considering what's best for the greater good of the society. Though sometimes risky, moral and upstanding individual citizens know that personal sacrifices must sometimes be made for others. They responsibly understand that there may be times in life when others win and they lose. This mature attitude changes when victim thinking exists. Consequently, the individual concludes that they must primarily fend for themselves and allow others to do the same. Our culture encourages us to think, "If it's me or you that has to survive, it's going to be me!" We will do whatever is necessary to avoid becoming victims, and feel justified as a matter of personal survival.

This mentality promotes serious crime within our society. Criminals are people looking out for their own interests and not the interests of those they victimize. We never hear reports of modern-day "Robin Hood" criminals motivated by a sense of righteousness and their compassion for those less fortunate. Crime and all forms of immorality ultimately happen as a result of selfish motives stemming from a need to protect one's self from some form of victimization.

A House Divided

In years past, basic and common interpretations of Biblical, moral, and Constitutional law unified various people groups, despite their cultural, ethnic, and political differences. But today that is no longer the case. It is becoming increasingly difficult to unite people based upon common values and agreed upon underlying moral principles. As a result, more and more socio-ideological movements are being created and division between people groups is inevitable. With each additional new movement spawned, division between people groups increases, becoming more difficult, if not impossible to reconcile.

With increased socio-political and socio-ideological movements, more attention is being given to normal events in society that have become quite controversial because they are driven and subjectively defined by feelings, sentiments, and emotions. The 2016 and 2020 Presidential election were the most cantankerous elections in my lifetime, and maybe in American history. The level of disrespect and dishonor demonstrated by both sides of the aisle was unbelievable and continues to this day. We recently witnessed the saga between Jussie Smollett and the Chicago Police Department concerning Jussie's alleged victimization by two black men wearing MAGA hats. We've heard reports of others being brutally assaulted for wearing MAGA hats.

We recently witnessed what was believed to be a white supremacist, neo-Nazi rally in Charleston, West Virginia. More and more lawsuits are being filed against Christian businesses and faith-based institutions for not supporting lifestyle choices that contradict their religious beliefs. We see Muslims profiled because of their dress and Black and Brown people still being profiled because of their skin color. We're seeing a growing backlash against white men with greater catch-all accusations of *white privilege* that have not been comprehensively defined.

With such growing division in our nation, we all lose no matter what side we choose. Why? Because every kingdom divided against itself is brought to desolation, and every city or house divided against itself will not stand. (Matthew 12:25). This sobering verse of ancient wisdom from Scripture reminds us of the catastrophic outcome of division. A radical course correction is needed now as victim mentality grows and is tearing our beloved nation apart.

Victims and Their Lawsuits

Today we are seeing a record number of lawsuits being filed in our nation. An estimated 15 million civil lawsuits are filed each year in the United States.[9] A significant number of these suits are frivolous, having been filed by people who are simply looking for easy money. Many people wait for, and never pass up a good opportunity to file a lawsuit. Those who are not seeking to sue others must be concerned about the possibility of being sued. The excessive use of our legal system can be traced back to citizens who suffer from high levels of victim mentality.

The basis for any lawsuit is to seek justice for a person who feels that they have been victimized. Whether the lawsuit deals with personal injury, property damage, breach of contract, or a custody battle, a lawsuit is filed by a person who perceives that another individual has wronged them in some way. When

[9] "Infographic: Lawsuits in America," Common Good, http://www.commongood.org/blog/entry/infographic-lawsuits-in-america

"With such growing division in
our nation, we all lose
no matter what side
we choose."

legitimate wrong is done, justice must be served. In each case, the plaintiff acts as the victim. Our multibillion-dollar legal industry thrives and profits on victim thinking.

Victims' Fears Drive Insurance

The insurance industry is one of the most lucrative industries in the world. Insurance policies covering our health, life, property, and vehicles have become an essential part of our lives. Regardless of the type of insurance offered, companies are in the business of selling protection to people who want to avoid becoming victims. Insurance companies market the need for protection, not only from unforeseen disastrous incidents, but also as a means of protection to defend people and businesses against lawsuits.

In some cases, our government mandates insurance coverage because of the likelihood of litigation. Purchasing car insurance is mandatory preparation for a future occasion in which you will become a victim of some unfortunate tragedy. Insurance coverage is the well-financed, strategic anticipation of victimization. Insurance cultivates victim mentality by reminding us it's just a matter of time before we become a victim.

Victims All Around the Issue of Race

The greatest affect of living in a hostile world that promotes victimization can be seen in matters concerning race. Culturally speaking, race generally refers to a group of people with common inherited features that distinguish them from other people groups. Race is an accepted social construct and is not a biological

"Insurance coverage is the well-financed, strategic anticipation of victimization."

reality. Only one human species or race exists to which every human belongs.

Throughout history, victim thinking has caused some racial groups to perceive other racial groups as threats to their existence. Because of this, some people groups have sought to oppress others, believing the opposite group to be in some way inferior to them. Victim thinking within the oppressive group causes them to marginalize the oppressed group. The people in the oppressed group then retaliate by perceiving themselves as victims of injustice. As this cycle continues racism occurs. Ultimately, racism is defined by unfortunate and misconstrued perceptions and attitudes about other people groups that result from victim mentality.

Unfortunately, racism persists today throughout the world among more than five thousand ethnic groups of people. Racism cannot be limited to Blacks and Whites in America, though historical racial encounters between the two groups are well known. If we look carefully, we can see how victim thinking has shaped race relations between Blacks and Whites throughout American history, and continues to affect the behavior of both groups of people today.

Slavery's Aftershocks Continue to Be Felt

Historians have traced the start of slavery back to 1619 in the North American colony of Jamestown, Virginia.[10] There the first African slaves were traded for food and supplies and used to provide labor for the growing tobacco, rice, and indigo industries

[10] "SlaveryinAmerica,"History.com,http://www.history.com/topics/black-history/slavery.

in America. As the colonies began to grow, the need for more slaves increased. African slaves in particular became essential to the economic foundation of this new, emerging nation. To control their behavior, slaves were prohibited from learning to read and write. They lived under tight restrictions often resulting in brutal beatings and even death.

In time, African slaves revolted and attempted to escape to obtain their freedom. This led to many incidents of Whites killing Blacks and Blacks killing Whites. By the mid-nineteenth century, the debate over slavery would partially fuel the American Civil War, resulting in the freedom of four million slaves. On January 1, 1863, President Abraham Lincoln officially declared freedom for all slaves in every state. Although the Civil War ended, the battle for freedom and equality was far from over. The Thirteenth Amendment adopted in 1865 officially abolished slavery, but Blacks would face significant challenges concerning equality for many years to come, and in some ways, still today.

Harder Than We Thought: Mental Struggle for Racial Equality

Although granted rights under the Thirteenth and Fourteenth Amendments, those rights often went ignored or simply denied throughout America. Congressional legislation did not instantly change the mentalities of American citizens concerning racial equality. Sentiments of white supremacy and black inferiority lingered across the nation, giving birth to racist organizations such as the Ku Klux Klan. The racism and discrimination that began during slavery persisted for the next one hundred years and lead to the Civil Rights Movement of the 1960s.

I have briefly and basically highlighted this historical information about slavery, not for the purpose of perpetually condemning white people or stirring the emotions of black people. The history of American slavery presents us with a relevant case study of the extraordinary power of victim mentality. Concerning racism, victim thinking encourages one race to believe it is superior to another race in order to protect itself from some perceived threat. This threat is often related to insecurity or fear, acted out in the form of oppression. At least to some degree, victim mentality among white people in the mid-nineteenth century caused them to oppress African slaves. Still today, some white people (certainly not all) continue to perpetuate some forms of systemic oppression and injustice in American culture.

On the other hand, we also see within the black community vestiges of victim thinking in the minds of those oppressed. Humbly speaking, I believe that black people–my own people–have developed victim thinking in response to the historical injustices we have experienced as a people group. Although seemingly justified because of the numerous atrocities of the past, many Blacks have developed deep resentment and hatred toward Whites. Black people have often retaliated with hate crimes against white people in response to the hate crimes white people have committed against them.

Still today, many Blacks remain embittered about the events that have happened to our ancestors at the hands of white people. Some Blacks believe white people who weren't even born and served no part in slavery owe them some form of restitution. They feel entitled to special benefits to even the score. Some pro-Black organizations and politicians strive to rally black people around their common pains and memories of past victimization.

“The history of American slavery presents us with a relevant case study of the extraordinary power of victim mentality.”

Within black America, I see strong evidence that our people group has not fully recovered from the effects of slavery, and are still greatly affected by historical slavery, racism, and discrimination. Much of what gets labeled as black-on-black crime proves to be a lack of value within the black community regarding the sanctity of black lives, much like the lack of value for black lives during the era of slavery. While Black America shouts to White America, "Black lives matter!" we're often left wondering if black lives even matter to black lives, because of all the violence we see toward each other.

I also believe that the rate of Black abortions prove a lack of value for black lives within the black community. It is painfully true that black people are presently doing to each other what white slave owners did in the 1800s. Infidelity and abandonment continue to destroy the cohesiveness of the nuclear black family. Each of these issues strongly suggest victim thinking remains prevalent within the black community.

I know this subject is extremely sensitive and somewhat painful as well as controversial to address, but racism holds a significant role in American history and America's present. Though I am not qualified or able to comprehensively address the subject of racism, I can identify how victim thinking fuels racism. Throughout my years of study, I have never heard anyone adequately address how victim mentality unceasingly serves as a catalyst for racism. I hope to see more discussions on racial equality while taking victim mentality into consideration.

Are You Willing to Change Your Heart and Mind?

Despite all that has happened and is happening in America, we are unable to change the past or change the hearts of other people. We can however, change our future outlook by first changing our own hearts and minds. Unfortunately, I don't believe racism will ever end because people are born with severe character flaws and hearts that are inherently sinful. We also tend to perpetuate racism through our own ignorance about other races. And yet, healing must take place.

No amount of apologies or restitution can undo crimes of the past committed against other races. Nothing can wipe away the pain of the Holocaust for the Jewish people. Yet, I sincerely believe the necessary healing can take place by identifying and eliminating victim thinking, even as we strive to take concrete steps to improve equality in our nation. To combat the harmful effects of racism, all of us must first seek to eliminate victim thinking in our own lives, be liberated from the mentality of defeat, and put forth earnest effort to rise above injustice with a new attitude.

CHAPTER THIRTEEN

Family: A Hotbed for Victim Mentality

As a Pastor, I have counseled hundreds of individuals concerning a wide range of family related challenges. These challenges include personal difficulties, as well as marriage, parenting, and extended family issues. I am convinced that most family problems such as arguments, divorce, and abandonment can be traced back to victim thinking. My intent is not to offer comprehensive pastoral insight for each of these struggles, but to offer a brief overview of how victim thinking is connected to these common problems in families.

Divorce: The Cause or the Effect?

Concerning divorce, we must ask the question, "Is divorce the result of a cause, or is it the result of an effect in marriage?" By asking this question, we can consider if divorce is an outcome based solely on a spouse's behavior (a cause), or if it is an outcome based upon some deeper, underlying, unresolved issue (an effect) within a spouse's heart or mind. Can a person's mentality–in this case a victim mentality–be a factor in promoting divorce? I say it is.

I believe that the bond of love and unity in marriage is so strong, that aside from a significant issue like sexual misconduct, breaking this bond requires a force much greater than stressed schedules, financial pressures, or differing opinions. Some of these issues exist in relationships before couples tie the knot and can be easily resolved. In contrast, victim mentality and its effects are not easily resolved.

We cannot dismiss the serious impact of victim thinking on the dissolution of a marriage. Divorce should be avoided if at all possible, but can sometimes be necessary due to instances of abuse or infidelity. In many cases, a husband and wife sincerely care for each other, but conclude that they cannot continue in their marriage if one of them perceives that their needs are not being met. Although this claim may be valid, I consider it to be the direct result of victim thinking. The individual with unmet needs perceives that they are being deprived of something that they are due and deserve. Labeling them as a victim may sound harsh or insensitive, but allow me to explain.

Love is the primary essential component in marriage. Although we culturally associate love with an emotional experience, that is not an accurate reflection of the true nature

"We cannot dismiss the serious impact of victim thinking on the dissolution of a marriage."

of love. Love can best be defined as total giving–total giving of one's life, time, attention, money, etc., to the person they love. Selfishness and self-centeredness are incompatible with true love.

Because love involves total giving, when true love exists within a marriage, the husband is only concerned about his wife's needs and not his own. Likewise, she is only concerned about his needs and not her own. The moment either of them turns their focus away from their spouse and toward themselves, they step into the role of a victim and immediately redefine and greatly weaken their marriage. The process of divorce usually begins here, long before a legal document can be presented and signed. In this scenario, communication, money, or differences of opinion do not represent the real problem. The real problem stems from a victim mentality.

Even years after infidelity occurred, couples who choose to continue in the marriage often struggle with resentment, which is another product of victim thinking. Many years after the unfortunate crisis, the infraction periodically resurfaces in their minds and conversations. Sometimes it resurfaces as a thought or occasional statement, just to remind their spouse of the injustice they experienced through their actions. The future health of the marriage is constantly threatened by a past experience of victimization. As a result, the historical injustice becomes the victim lense through which their spouse and marriage will always be seen and defined.

I'm Not Talking to You!

Lack of communication in a relationship breeds victim thinking. A primary characteristic of passive-aggressive behavior is to withhold communication. This relationship damaging practice uses covert ways to express feelings, and is typically used as a weapon of retaliation to frustrate, manipulate, and control another individual.

A victim quickly recognizes the possibility of getting back at others, not only by what they can do, but also by what they won't do for them or won't say to them. The *silent treatment* is a powerful weapon in the arsenal of a victim thinker. Because it is easier to implement than direct confrontation, a victim thinker often prefers this behavior. To them, their unwillingness to communicate is rationally justified by victim thinking.

Abandonment Cultivates Guaranteed Victim Mentality

Abandonment causes considerable lifelong damage to families, especially to children. Children rely on both parents, but primarily their fathers to help them define and discover their identity in their formative years of life. Parents must primarily teach their children morals and values, and help them distinguish between what is right and what is wrong. Children derive their self-esteem directly from their parents' affirmation and celebration of them. When a parent abandons a child, severe psychological and emotional damage occurs, which often results in feelings of guilt, fear, worthlessness, and rejection.

These unwanted sentiments all but guarantee that a child will live its life as a victim. The abandonment they experienced as a child becomes their set of victim lenses. They usually develop a deeply rooted belief and fear that others will also abandon them in life, which relegates them to a victim mentality. To avoid being hurt or disappointed, they would rather live in isolation than develop intimate and meaningful relationships with others. They will possibly live the entirety of their life believing they are a victim of abandonment, which will potentially damage all future relationships.

You Love Him Best: Victim Mentality and Siblings

Victim mentality often causes great strain on relationships between siblings and contributes to sibling rivalries. We saw this in the story of Joseph's family in an earlier chapter. What's known as *middle child syndrome* is possible in families with three or more children, and often exemplifies victim mentality among siblings.

The firstborn child tends to emerge with great confidence and understanding that they have inherited a degree of favored status by simply being born first. They often intentionally or unintentionally relate to their siblings with an attitude of superiority. As the latest addition to the family, the youngest sibling naturally garners more attention and time from the parents because they represent closure to the parents' child producing years. Being *the baby of the family* carries great sentiment.

Middle children find themselves in position to observe the special attention and favored status naturally given to the oldest and youngest siblings. Consequently, they can soon develop a victim mentality and feel compelled or pressured to do something exceptional to be appreciated and noticed. Their victim status grows if their parents fail to celebrate them as much as the older and younger siblings. The middle child silently becomes a victim

“The *silent treatment* is a powerful weapon in the arsenal of a victim thinker.”

as they struggle to find their place of significance within the family structure.

Parents greatly impact a child's development and mentality, but siblings do as well. Those with siblings initially spend more time with them than anyone else in life. Your experiences with your brothers and sisters, as well as the order in which you were born, can be significant factors in the shaping of your mentality.

Victim Thinking and Singles Are a Terrible Match

Singles may not experience the family issues previously mentioned, but do deal with relationship dynamics associated with victim thinking as well. Singles are not immune to relationship issues, and must protect themselves against pervasive victim thinking.

Unmarried people sometimes formulate inaccurate or negative conclusions about themselves as a result of not being in a committed relationship. Conclusions such as, "I am not attractive." "No one wants me." or "Something must be wrong with me." often circulate within the mind of a single person. A single person with a victim mentality who sees their friends getting married, may be haunted by thoughts such as, "When will my time come?" or "My biological clock is ticking." These thoughts can be the seeds that will eventually produce a harvest of victim thinking, which commonly leads to some form of discouragement or depression.

Victim mentality concerning dating relationships can affect a single in one of two ways. I have witnessed some singles become depressed and lose all hope of ever being involved in a committed relationship, and as a result they become careless about their appearance. Their physical appearance becomes less of a priority as they cease putting forth effort to attract the opposite sex. They simply give up. They wallow in self-pity and withdraw from social interaction with peers. Unexpectedly, an eligible candidate emerges, but the single-turned-victim disqualified himself or herself from eligibility.

The second effect of victim mentality on some singles is desperation. Because their *biological clock* is ticking, they sometimes lower their moral standards for a relationship, allowing almost anyone to be in a relationship with them. Compromising their moral standards sometimes result in an unplanned pregnancy, because their victim thinking pressured them into abandoning their standards and values in relationships.

Your Past Has Passed!

In each of these examples, a Zero Victim Mentality can liberate individuals from victim thinking. By seeing their unfortunate experiences through Zero Victim lenses, each of them can be healed and ultimately overcome their victim status.

Imagine the calamity of you attempting to drive forward while only looking in the rearview mirror. What's behind you should be glanced at periodically, but not fixated upon. Your past experiences significantly influence your present perceptions and future possibilities. In counseling, we refer to this projection. Going back to our victim lenses analogy, past experiences often determine the tint and type of lenses through which you see.

To develop a Zero Victim Mentality, you must carefully consider your history, your beliefs, values, presuppositions, superstitions, etc., and question the validity of each of them. In your efforts to discard victim thinking, you must realize that some unsuitable ideals from your past must be eliminated if you intend to reach your destination.

"Your past experiences significantly influence your present perceptions and future possibilities."

CHAPTER FOURTEEN

Five Lessons About Zero Victim Mentality from the Greatest Teacher of All

We established in chapter three that the world is a hostile place. At various times in our lives, all of us encounter people or circumstances that work against us. Intentionally or unintentionally, people usually cause us to experience those negative circumstances. An identity thief victimizes people intentionally–a drunk driver unintentionally. Either way, people with a Zero Victim Mentality choose to act and not react to those circumstances.

On my spiritual and intellectual quest to better understand Zero Victim Mentality, I discovered the Bible to be the greatest resource on how to eliminate victim thinking. Jesus leads as the greatest example I could find of someone who modeled Zero Victim thinking. I would like to share with you five important lessons I learned from His example.

Zero Victim Lesson #1: Don't Seek Revenge

In dealing with an enemy, most of us prefer to *take them out* before they can *take us out*. If they bring harm to us first, we usually avenge ourselves by retaliating in some way, and then justify our reaction because of what they did to us. As children, whenever another child injured us, our playground code of ethics executed justice by seeking *an eye for an eye and a tooth for a tooth*. Little did we know the Bible mentions this form of justice. Note the words of Jesus in His Sermon on the Mount:

> *"You have heard the law that says the punishment must match the injury: 'An eye for an eye, and a tooth for a tooth.' But I say, do not resist an evil person! If someone slaps you on the right cheek, offer the other cheek also. If you are sued in court and your shirt is taken from you, give your coat, too. If a soldier demands that you carry his gear for a mile, carry it two miles..."* (Matthew 5:38-41).

Here we see Jesus introduce a new response to injury and injustice. He introduces the response of an individual who exercises Zero Victim thinking. If a person strikes you physically, don't strike back. If a person sues you, don't countersue. If you have been forced into manual labor, don't rebel. This response would be considered weak, irrational, and even insane in today's culture. From childhood, we learn to defend ourselves and never allow anyone to take advantage of us.

But if you look carefully, you'll see Jesus teach potential victims how to take control of our situation by first changing our mentality. When slapped on the face, instead of perceiving ourselves as victims of abuse, Jesus instructs us to victoriously rise above the situation with a new attitude–to demonstrate exceptional strength and self-control able to willingly receive a blow on the other cheek. At that moment, the victim becomes greater than their abuser and displays a mentality that cannot be defeated.

If you lose your shirt in a lawsuit, instead of perceiving yourself as a victim, voluntarily offer your coat. The plaintiff cannot take what you as the defendant are willing to freely give to them. If you are forced to perform manual labor, instead of identifying yourself as a victim, readily offer to work twice as hard. With a Zero Victim Mentality, you cannot be enslaved.

Jesus was not of course, justifying the mistreatment of anyone. Nor did He say we should condone or embrace injustice. He was introducing a mentality that perceives the situation differently, and liberates the potential victim from a mentality of defeat and victimization.

Zero Victim Lesson #2: Love Your Enemies

Everyone has a different definition of love. Instead of explaining what love is, Jesus shows us love in action.

"You have heard the law that says, 'Love your neighbor' and hate your enemy. But I say, love your enemies! Pray for those who persecute you! (Matthew 5:43-44).

We naturally love likeable people and hate those who harm us. That would be a normal and expected emotional response. However, when we carefully consider Jesus' words, we see He does not refer to an emotional response, but to an intentional decision–a decision that results from a specific and unique way of thinking.

Despite the harm we experience at the hands of those who are against us, Jesus encourages a willful response to love and pray for them. This kind of response can only occur from individuals who do not perceive themselves as victims of their enemies and persecutors. The decision to love and pray for your enemies is derived from a Zero Victim Mentality, and empowers you as a potential victim to take control over their actions.

Many people's lives are controlled by the unfortunate memories their enemies and oppressors created. They then spend the remainder of their lives dealing with mental and emotional wounds. Think of all the people in your past who hurt you and persecuted you. How did you respond in each of those circumstances? How would the outcomes of those circumstances have been different if you had loved your enemies and prayed for them? When practicing this lesson, in the heat of the moment, you may initially feel like a loser. But truthfully, your decision to respond differently than expected–to repay evil with good, instead of evil with evil–will give you the upper hand in every situation. Zero Victim thinking will always give you the upper hand.

"Many people's lives are controlled by the unfortunate memories their enemies and oppressors created."

Zero Victim Lesson #3: Treat People the Way You Want to Be Treated

Almost everyone has heard the Golden Rule, but most people may be unaware that the principle originated with Jesus.

> *"Do to others whatever you would like them to do to you. This is the essence of all that is taught in the law and the prophets"* (Matthew 7:12).

To develop a Zero Victim Mentality you must spend quality time thinking about how you want people to treat you. Would you like to be treated with respect, kindness, and mercy? As you formulate these preferred standards for yourself, Jesus taught that you must first implement them in your treatment of others.

Oftentimes, people mistreat other people because they never considered how they would like to be treated. When you live out a Zero Victim Mentality, you define the standards for your relationships. Once these standards have been resolutely defined, your objective is to place others before yourself. In this process, you cannot become a victim because you have removed yourself from the equation. The Golden Rule negates victim thinking by shifting your focus toward serving others instead of contemplating your own pain. Ultimately, victim mentality is an expression of selfishness and self-centeredness.

Zero Victim Lesson #4: Show Mercy

The Golden Rule lesson concerning Zero Victim thinking focuses on how an individual relates to others. Jesus' teaching about the Good Samaritan focuses on the prioritization of others.

"The Golden Rule negates victim thinking by shifting your focus toward serving others instead of contemplating your own pain."

People with a Zero Victim Mentality seek to put others ahead of themselves.

> *A Jewish man was traveling on a trip from Jerusalem to Jericho, and he was attacked by bandits. They stripped him of his clothes, beat him up, and left him half dead beside the road.*
>
> *By chance a priest came along. But when he saw the man lying there, he crossed to the other side of the road and passed him by. A Temple assistant walked over and looked at him lying there, but he also passed by on the other side.*
>
> *Then a despised Samaritan came along, and when he saw the man, he felt compassion for him. Going over to him, the Samaritan soothed his wounds with olive oil and wine and bandaged them. Then he put the man on his own donkey and took him to an inn, where he took care of him. The next day he handed the innkeeper two silver coins, telling him, 'Take care of this man. If his bill runs higher than this, I'll pay you the next time I'm here.'*
>
> *"Now which of these three would you say was a neighbor to the man who was attacked by bandits?" Jesus asked. The man replied, "The one who showed him mercy"* (Luke 10:30-37).

This story tells of a man identified as "a despised Samaritan" who showed compassion to a victim of injustice. It is significant to note that the name of this despised Samaritan goes unmentioned, so the reader would understand that he is not the central character in the story.

Upon finding a man who was a victim of injustice, the Samaritan made a decision–a decision motivated by compassion, that went above and beyond minimal care for the man who had been robbed and wounded–a man who happened to be his racial enemy. The Samaritan immediately dressed the victim's wounds, transported him to an inn, and paid for the cost of the victim's care. Furthermore, he established an unlimited line of credit with the innkeeper to cover any additional care needed.

Rather than focus on the victim, the story focuses on the unnamed, despised Samaritan who demonstrated Zero Victim thinking. Clearly unconcerned about being imposed upon or being taken advantage of, the Samaritan is not only the main character, but is the hero of the story.

How many times do we see people in need and refuse to help them because we're afraid they'll take advantage of our precious time and resources? We often refuse to help others who are victims, to prevent ourselves from becoming victims of inconvenience and loss of revenue. An individual with a Zero Victim Mentality shows mercy toward others without fear of personal loss. The Samaritan focused on alleviating the victimization of the true victim, without even considering the potential of his own ill treatment.

Zero Victim Lesson #5: God Does Help Those Who Help Themselves!

From another one of Jesus' teachings, we see some truth to the old adage, "God helps those who help themselves." Jesus often portrayed a partnership model between God and people, as opposed to God doing everything for people in need. At times, individuals in Scripture participated in their miracles. Consider the man Jesus healed at the pool of Bethesda:

> *Inside the city, near the Sheep Gate, was the pool of Bethesda, with five covered porches. Crowds of sick people–blind, lame, or paralyzed–lay on the porches. One of the men lying there had been sick for thirty-eight years. When Jesus saw him and knew he had been ill for a long time, he asked him, "Would you like to get well?"*
>
> *"I can't, sir," the sick man said, "for I have no one to put me into the pool when the water bubbles up. Someone else always gets there ahead of me."*
>
> *Jesus told him, "Stand up, pick up your mat, and walk!" Instantly, the man was healed! He rolled up his sleeping mat and began walking!* (John 5:2-9).

Considering his actions, or really, the lack thereof, the sick man clearly possessed a mentality of defeat from which he desperately needed to be liberated. Four key factors contributed to his victim mentality:

1. **Wrong Environment and Wrong Relationships** - The sick man resided in the company of sick people for thirty-eight years. I do not want to come across as being insensitive to people experiencing health challenges, but this man lived in an environment for thirty-eight years where sickness was normal. When everyone in a community suffers from the same negative condition, dysfunctional behavior becomes normalized, and functional behavior becomes abnormal. When individuals live in an environment where undesirable conditions such as poverty, broken

“When everyone in a community suffers from the same negative condition, dysfunctional behavior becomes normalized, and functional behavior becomes abnormal.”

families, and crime are normal, those individuals tend to become accustomed to these environments and usually see themselves as victims of their surroundings.

2. **Time Delay** - Over the years, the sick man had become programmed for delay. He never anticipated nor prepared for a specific moment when his condition would change and he would be free from his infirmity. He became a victim of time by becoming complacent or "stuck" in his condition. The sick man became accustomed to waiting indefinitely, instead of taking control of his circumstances. In most cases, ongoing deferred hope eventually becomes hopelessness.

3. **Lack of Desire** - Jesus asked the sick man, "Would you like to get well?" The man never answered Jesus' question. We want him to say with confidence, "Yes! I want to be made well!" Yet he does not appear to have firm resolve to be healed. Victim mentality encourages tolerance and acceptance of undesired circumstances, which over time, breaks an individual's will to change. In some cases, victims actually prefer the comfort of the familiar, choosing to keep things the way they are, as opposed to the discomfort of making things better.

4. **Excuses** - Though the sick man did not respond by answering, "Yes!" he did respond with three excuses that justified his condition: 1) he didn't have anyone to help him; 2) he needed to wait for the water to be stirred before jumping into the healing waters; and 3) someone else jumps into the water before him (the people believed that when the water began to stir, the first person to jump into the pool would be healed). Victim thinking perpetuates the

"A Zero Victim thinker endeavors to live life from the inside out and not from the outside in."

idea that someone else–a parent, spouse, boss, church, or the government–must do for you what you are unable to do for yourself. This man believed that someone getting into the pool ahead of him was responsible for his unchanging condition, making him a "loser" to those competing against him. As a victim, their win meant his loss.

Anyone Can Go from Victim to Victorious

Jesus responded to the sick man with simple instructions of faith and self-initiative: "Stand up, pick up your mat, and walk!" Despite all the reasons the sick man offered to justify his elongated condition, Jesus challenged his victim thinking by telling him to take initiative in participating in his miracle. A Zero Victim Mentality does not demand entitlements, blame others, or justify unacceptable conditions, but instead takes personal initiative to change those conditions by doing what must be done.

A Zero Victim thinker endeavors to live life from the inside out and not from the outside in. The uncontrollable world around us will never cease to create victims. Attempting to control the world will only prove to be frustrating and a waste of time. The only real control we have in life is control of what happens within us–not what happens to us or around us.

Individuals who have mastered their thoughts and emotions, stand the best chance of living the highest possible quality of life, by developing a mentality that liberates them from defeat. When you develop a Zero Victim Mentality, you cannot lose in life, no matter what happens to you.

CHAPTER FIFTEEN
On to Your Victory!

I wrote this book to equip you with the tools necessary to control what seems to be uncontrollable outcomes. By learning to successfully control your mentality, the way you see and thus experience life will change. You must never forget that your life is *your life,* and that you alone must take control of it. You sit in the driver's seat. No matter how much others care for you and support you, your life will not change until you decide to change it.

Individuals often blame others for hindering them from reaching their potential in life. Children fault their parents. Students blame their teachers. Employees blame their bosses. Women blame men. Citizens blame politicians. Sometimes, black people blame white people, and poor people blame rich people. Decade after decade, the blame cycle of victim thinking continues. Victims are people who live perceiving some person or group is holding them back.

My Zero Victim Mentality helped me reach a critical conclusion. Many years ago, I determined that I love the people in my life too much to not do what I know I have been called to do in life. I determined that I would never allow the time to come, when I would blame them for hindering me or holding me back from my calling. I determined that I would never allow myself to become a victim and jeopardize my relationship with them because of offense. I am not encouraging anyone to become a lawless individual who disrespects and disregards civil, professional, parental, or spiritual authority. Having a Zero Victim Mentality does not mean becoming a rebel.

Don't Ignore the Problem—Solve It!

We typically think of problems as difficulties or complications. We often get depressed about problems. We cry, quit, and fight about problems and ignore problems, but rarely confront them head-on to solve them. Zero Victim thinkers do not bury their heads in the sand by sleeping or drinking in an attempt to forget about their problems.

I have heard positive thinkers and people of faith say that we should not talk about our problems, but only talk about the solution. Consider all your years of education. Did you ever score well on an exam by not carefully studying the problems? Most likely you did not, because accurate solutions can only be discovered through accurate analysis of the existing problem.

Be a Landlord, Not a Tenant

A common misunderstanding about problems is that they are always negative. Every problem asks the question, "What's wrong

"You must never forget
that your life is *your life,*
and that you alone must
take control of it."

in this situation?" Simply put, a problem represents something in need of correction or repair. Repair comes by first asking the right questions. Because life is filled with problems, people who do well in life are those who ask intelligent questions about their problems and become great problem solvers.

Friends, I want to challenge you to have a problem with your problems. Victim thinking must become a problem to you. You must determine that thoughts of victimization will no longer be problems that plague your life, but instead issues for you to solve once and for all. Zero Victim thinking begins by identifying issues that need to be resolved. This exercise is not intended to produce problem consciousness, but to move you toward responsible action in dealing with those problems effectively.

As long as you conclude that a problem belongs to someone else, it will never be solved. Tenants don't deal with property problems the same way landlords do. Tenants are usually passive whereas landlords are aggressive because of ownership. Tenants think, "That's his problem!" Landlords think, "That's my problem!" I want to encourage you to deal with offenses and injustices as a landlord and property owner and not as a tenant.

Here are three important conclusions to remember when solving the problem of victimization in your life:

1. Until you have a problem with your problems, you will always have problems.
2. Things that create a problem for you must become a problem to you. You must move from defense to offense in life. You cannot solve what you are unwilling to address.

"Simply put, a problem represents something in need of correction or repair."

3. Once a problem really becomes a problem to you, you'll solve it. You'll never solve what you tolerate and are willing to coexist with.

Changing the Way You Think

Paul the apostle had many opportunities to develop victim thinking. You could say that he had many problems in life and in ministry. He experienced more persecution and injustice than most of us ever will. Listen to Paul's account of the injustice he faced:

> *Are they servants of Christ? I know I sound like a madman, but I have served him far more! I have worked harder, been put in prison more often, been whipped times without number, and faced death again and again. Five different times the Jewish leaders gave me thirty-nine lashes. Three times I was beaten with rods. Once I was stoned. Three times I was shipwrecked. Once I spent a whole night and a day adrift at sea. I have traveled on many long journeys. I have faced danger from rivers and from robbers. I have faced danger from my own people, the Jews, as well as from the Gentiles. I have faced danger in the cities, in the deserts, and on the seas. And I have faced danger from men who claim to be believers but are not. I have worked hard and long, enduring many sleepless nights. I have been hungry and thirsty and have often gone without food. I have shivered in the cold, without enough clothing to keep me warm.*
>
> *Then, besides all this, I have the daily burden of my concern for all the churches. Who is weak without my feeling*

that weakness? Who is led astray, and I do not burn with anger?

If I must boast, I would rather boast about the things that show how weak I am. God, the Father of our Lord Jesus, who is worthy of eternal praise, knows I am not lying. When I was in Damascus, the governor under King Aretas kept guards at the city gates to catch me. I had to be lowered in a basket through a window in the city wall to escape from him (2 Corinthians 11:23-33).

Despite the extreme difficulties and hardships Paul faced, he gives us the secret of how to deal with them with a Zero Victim Mentality.

Don't copy the behavior and customs of this world, but let God transform you into a new person by changing the way you think (Romans 12:2).

Here Paul explains that we must allow God to transform us by changing the way we think. That is my prayer for you–that God will revolutionize your life for the better, not only by changing your circumstances, but also by changing the way you think about your circumstances, just as He did for Paul.

Your universal victory in every circumstance of life is based upon you changing from the inside-out. As you develop a Zero Victim Mentality, you will indeed liberate yourself from the mentality of defeat and overcome any injustice against you just as Paul did. On to your freedom! On to your victory! I'm cheering for you!

APPENDIX

From Victim to Victorious in Christ

Among many responsibilities, I am primarily a pastor and Bible teacher. My greatest passion in life is teaching people God's Word. As a pastor, I am deeply saddened whenever I see people struggle with problems that can easily be solved. I desire to help people avoid these unnecessary difficulties in life by obtaining and applying the wisdom of God.

According to Scripture, every individual is created in God's image and likeness, making people superior and distinct from all other forms of life. Our existence is not an accident or result of random selection. God intentionally made us on purpose, for a purpose!

God's wisdom can only be found in the Bible. I am convinced that the Bible is God's owner's manual for us. I consider it the best roadmap available for navigating through a hostile world, where we constantly face unpredictable circumstances and insurmountable obstacles.

Although each of us is capable of making intelligent decisions, I discovered that developing a Zero Victim Mentality involves much more than making a series of rational choices. Although we can marginally improve our lives by making a concerted effort to do so, positive transformation ultimately entails a spiritual reality that informs our thoughts, and is reflected in our physical actions. Paul the apostle explains this process in his letter to the Romans:

> *Don't copy the behavior and customs of this world, but let God transform you into a new person by changing the way you think. Then you will learn to know God's will for you, which is good and pleasing and perfect* (Romans 12:2).

From this verse we see that mental transformation–in our case, the development of a Zero Victim Mentality–can only be accomplished through God. As God changes the way we think, our lives are transformed and improved from the inside-out. Despite what external challenges you may be facing, your life can and will change from within with God's help! I would like to briefly share four spiritual principles from the Bible that will assist you in fully grasping the concept of Zero Victim Mentality.

Mankind Was Created to Be Like God

While various scientific theories exist regarding the origin of humans, the Bible reveals God creating heaven and earth and all of their contents, including mankind.

> *Then God said, "Let Us make man in Our image, according to Our likeness; let them have dominion over the fish of the sea, over the birds of the air, and over the cattle, over all the earth and over every creeping thing that creeps on the earth." So God created man in His own image; in the image of God He created him; male and female He created them. Then God blessed them, and God said to them, "Be fruitful and multiply; fill the earth and subdue it; have dominion over the fish of the sea, over the birds of the air, and over every living thing that moves on the earth"* (Genesis 1:26-28, NKJV).

Here we see that mankind was created to replicate God on earth, which distinguishes humans from all other creatures. As I mentioned before, mankind was made to be superior to other forms of life and was given authority over them. Having been made by God in His own image and likeness, man was originally perfect in spirit, mind, and body. A perfect God is only capable of creating things perfectly. He never makes a mistake! At the time of his creation, man's spirit contained the very life of God. His mentality was such that he thought like God, and even lived on earth physically free from sickness and disease.

Something Went Wrong

Because mankind was created in God's image and likeness, humans possess free will. Although God desires for people to use their free will to choose to be in relationship with Him, because their free will is *free*, they can also choose to not be in relationship with God. People can agree or disagree with God. Even when they mistakenly disagree with Him, God respects their *right* to be wrong. This holds true today. An individual's personal relationship with God is not forced, but is based upon his or her willing choice to pursue a relationship with God by humbly choosing to obey His Word.

Adam was the first man created. God gave him a specific instruction to follow concerning his life on earth. Then God graciously and lovingly warned Adam that if he failed to obey His instruction, there would be severe consequences.

> *Then the LORD God took the man and put him in the garden of Eden to tend and keep it. And the LORD God commanded the man, saying, "Of every tree of the garden you may freely eat; but of the tree of the knowledge of good and evil you shall not eat, for in the day that you eat of it you shall surely die"* (Genesis 2:15-17, NKJV).

Although Adam was perfect, he pridefully exercised his free will when he chose to disobey God's instruction.

> *So when the woman saw that the tree was good for food, that it was pleasant to the eyes, and a tree desirable to make one wise, she took of its fruit and ate. She also gave to her husband with her, and he ate* (Genesis 3:6, NKJV).

By disobeying God, Adam allied himself with God's adversary called Satan. As part of the consequences of Adam rebelling against God, His Spirit, nature, and character within Adam were destroyed, and Adam also lost God's mentality. Worst of all, Adam would be separated from God forever. Here is where victim thinking first began. Note Adam's response when confronted by God concerning his decision to disobey God:

> *And they heard the sound of the LORD God walking in the garden in the cool of the day, and Adam and his wife hid themselves from the presence of the LORD God among the trees of the garden.*
>
> *Then the LORD God called to Adam and said to him, "Where are you?"*
>
> *So he said, "I heard Your voice in the garden, and I was afraid because I was naked; and I hid myself."*
>
> *And He said, "Who told you that you were naked? Have you eaten from the tree of which I commanded you that you should not eat?"*
>
> *Then the man said, "The woman whom You gave to be with me, she gave me of the tree, and I ate"* (Genesis 3:8-12, NKJV).

After disobeying God, Adam experienced the negative emotions of fear and shame for the first time, which propelled him to blame both God and the woman for his rebellious behavior. Here we see the first instance of victim thinking and victim talk. As the biological father of all mankind, Adam's DNA was passed on to his offspring, who naturally inherited his victim mentality as their way of thinking and were also separated from God.

Still today, victim thinking rules as our default mentality. Overcoming this mental dilemma requires divine assistance and divine intervention. Only God can ultimately remove victim thinking. As He does, man can once again possess the mentality of God.

We Need to Be Rescued

God did not desire to leave mankind in this fallen condition. God did not create people to be separate from Him and to fail. Many years later, because of God's great love for people, He sent His Son, Jesus Christ, to rescue mankind and save people from the eternal consequences of Adam's failure to obey God.

> *And behold, you will conceive in your womb and bring forth a Son, and shall call His name JESUS* (Luke 1:31, NKJV).
>
> *And she will bring forth a Son, and you shall call His name JESUS, for He will save His people from their sins"* (Matthew 1:21, NKJV).

This verse of Scripture reveals why the title Savior refers to Jesus exclusively. He physically died to pay the penalty for Adam's disobedience to God. Jesus gives new life to those who believe in Him by restoring within them God's Spirit–the same Spirit Adam lost. Included in Jesus' rescue of mankind, is restoration of the image and likeness of God in those who believe in Him. Jesus empowers people to once again be like God and think like God, delivering them from eternal separation from God and from the bondage of victim thinking.

When people believe in Jesus as their Savior, their lives miraculously unite with His! Jesus begins to live within them by His Spirit, transforming them from the inside-out and giving them new life.

"Still today, victim thinking rules as our default mentality."

> *I have been crucified with Christ; it is no longer I who live, but Christ lives in me; and the life which I now live in the flesh I live by faith in the Son of God, who loved me and gave Himself for me* (Galatians 2:20, NKJV).

A supernatural and spiritual change happens in people as the old person "dies" and a new person is created in Christ. Once the old person is "dead," the individual who places their faith in Christ is no longer captive to the power sin and of victim thinking. Think about it. When was the last time you attended a funeral and heard the person in the casket complain about anything? Never! Why? Because dead people have no feelings, opinions, perceptions, or pains. Dead people are not victims! When the old you "dies" spiritually, so does your capacity to be offended, because you are dead to yourself but alive unto God.

How Can I Be Rescued?

The Bible tells us, in order to be rescued, we must humble ourselves by calling upon the Lord to rescue us.

> *And it shall come to pass that whoever calls on the name of the LORD shall be saved.* (Acts 2:21, NKJV).

The greatest day of my life was the day Jesus saved me! If you would like for Jesus to save you from eternal separation from God, from victim mentality, and from all of the other consequences of sinning against God, pray these words to God out loud, and mean them with all of your heart:

"The greatest day of
my life was the day
Jesus saved me!"

God, I admit that I am not perfect and have done many wrong things in life. I humbly admit I have sinned against you and I need Your help. Therefore, I'm asking You to please forgive me of my sins. I believe that You sent Your Son, Jesus, to rescue me, by dying on the Cross, and that He was raised from the dead on the third. So from this moment forward, I am giving my life to You, Jesus. I confess with my mouth and believe in my heart that You are now my Savior and my Lord. With Your help, I am willing to follow You alone by obeying Your written Word. I ask You to give me Your heart and to fill me with Your Holy Spirit, to empower me to be the person You died for me to become. I pray this in Your name. Amen!

You Can't Lose!

Congratulations! Friend, if you prayed this prayer sincerely and meant it with all your heart, God has already saved you and begun His transformation process in your life. You won't necessarily feel anything physically, but believe by faith that your salvation is true. God honors and responds to your faith! Now, go find a great church that will teach you God's Word and help you live as a faithful and true follower of Jesus Christ. I invite you to become part of the church I lead online at insightchurch.org.

Now that you have received Jesus as your Savior and Lord, observe just a few of the countless promises the Bible contains about you being victorious in all circumstances of life. As you become more like Christ, you will increasingly be liberated from the mentality of defeat, and be empowered to rise above any injustice with a new attitude!

And we know that all things work together for good to those who love God, to those who are the called according to His purpose (Romans 8:28, NKJV).

What then shall we say to these things? If God is for us, who can be against us? (Romans 8:31, NKJV).

But thanks be to God, who gives us the victory through our Lord Jesus Christ (1 Corinthians 15:57, NKJV).

I can do all things through Christ who strengthens me (Philippians 4:13, NKJV).

The Power of Love!

In studying Scripture, it is clear to see how much emphasis God places on the Biblical themes love, mercy, and forgiveness. As I have studied these more carefully, it seems as though God has a bigger problem with offended people than those who offend. Could it be that between the offender and the person offended, that the person offended is the bigger sinner? I believe so.

God is love. Listen to the apostle Paul describe the nature of love:

Love suffers long and is kind; love does not envy; love does not parade itself, is not puffed up; does not behave rudely, does not seek its own, is not provoked, thinks no evil; does not rejoice in iniquity, but rejoices in the truth; bears all things, believes all things, hopes all things, endures all things. Love never fails. But whether there are prophecies, they will fail; whether there are tongues, they will cease; whether there is knowledge, it will vanish away. (1 Corinthians 13:4-8 NKJV)

Because God is love, everywhere we read the word "love" we can replace it with "God." Now let's take another look at this passage of Scripture:

> *"God suffers long and is kind; God does not envy; God does not parade Himself, is not puffed up; [God] does not behave rudely, does not seek His own, is not provoked, thinks no evil; [God] does not rejoice in iniquity, but rejoices in the truth; [God] bears all things, believes all things, hopes all things, endures all things. God never fails..."*

Having been originally created in God's image, according to His likeness, if He is love, we are called to be lovers like Him. Let's read this passage once more, this time inserting personal pronouns to make it personal.

> *"I suffer long and I am kind; I do not envy; I do not parade myself, [and] I am not puffed up; I do not behave rudely, [I] do not seek my own, [I] am not provoked, [I] think no evil; [I] do not rejoice in iniquity, but [I] rejoice in the truth; [I] bear all things, [I] believe all things, [I] hope [the best] for all things, [I] endure all things. [I] never fail..."*

You may say, "That's impossible!" But through Christ and with the help of the Holy Spirit, this is exactly what God is calling each of us to be and to do–to love–to become individuals who are unoffendable, and do not consider themselves to be victims. These loving individuals are longsuffering with those who offend them. They do not envy those different from them. They do not put themselves or their feelings first. Even when other people are rude to them, they do not respond with rudeness. They are completely unselfish. They are not victims.

Loving people cannot be provoked into offense or victim thinking, and are incapable of even thinking evil of those who have possibly and legitimately hurt them. Lovers like God rejoice in truth, and not their emotions and feelings about what is true or untrue. These people are empowered by love to bear all things. They are capable of withstanding the toughest circumstances in life. No matter how disheartening the situation may seem, they believe and hope for the best outcome in all things, and endure to the very end. These people–Zero Victim people– never fail!

The apostle Peter continues:

> *And above all things have fervent love for one another, for "love will cover a multitude of sins."* (1 Peter 4:8 NKJV)

No matter what has been done to us or what injustice we've suffered, we are called to have fervent love toward others, including our enemies. Despite what they have done or could possibly do, genuine love–if applied by faith–is capable of covering any and all sins. Whenever I share this truth, I hear people say, "But you don't know what I've been through. You don't know the pain I suffered!" My response is this. The only innocent Man [Jesus Christ] to ever walk the face of the earth, suffered the greatest injustice ever known. He was brutally crucified and killed for the sins of other people, and not His own. No matter what's been done to any of us, the injustice of our victimization is incapable of surpassing the injustice Christ suffered for all people. That means any offense against us, less than our sins against Jesus is forgivable and reconcilable through the power of forgiveness and love.

God makes great provision by His mercy for people who sin against us. The individual who is incapable or unwilling to apply love to every offense is unlike God. If we won't forgive others, our Heavenly Father won't forgive us. Jesus tells us to pray to our Father God, "Forgive us for our tresspasses, as we forgive those who trespass against us."

Unfortunately, many Christians sincerely love Jesus and confess their desire to be like Him, but don't think and behave like the Jesus they claim love and follow. Zero Victim thinking is a product of true discipleship. Christians must continuously ask the question, "Did Jesus ever get offended?"

Jesus never commanded us to not make mistakes, but He does command us to forgive and love. Not offending other people is not a commandment in Scripture, but we are commanded to not be offended. That means the people who don't forgive and don't love, are greater transgressors than those who offend.

No matter how we attempt to justify our offenses and victimizations, if we're honest, we must admit that all of our frustrations and offenses with people are the result of victim thinking. Even if we believe our feelings are justified, victim thinking is at work in our minds. Victim thinkers are more concerned with changing other people and circumstances, than changing what they think and feel about those people and circumstances. Victim thinking is the springboard of all offense.

I'm thankful that God spends His energy thinking about His love for us and His mercy toward us, instead of our sins and offenses against Him.

"The only innocent Man
(Jesus Christ) to ever walk
the face of the earth,
suffered the greatest
injustice ever known."

> *For I will be merciful to their unrighteousness, and their sins and their lawless deeds I will remember no more."* (Hebrews 8:12 NKJV)

When we think and behave like God, it is very difficult to remain offended by pain, injustice, and victimizations you choose not to rehearse and remember. Think about this. The way Jesus thinks about us is what initially affords us salvation and relationship with Him. He does not wait for us to change our behavior, only the disposition of our heart toward Him. When an individual comes to faith in Christ, they don't always instantaneously behave better. But Jesus instantaneously changes the way He thinks about them, because they have declared Him to be Lord over their life. You could say the most difficult part of the deal is on the side of Jesus–changing the way He thinks about people like me who will undoubtedly continue to offend Him. Being righteous and doing what's right is always more difficult, and requires more effort than being unrighteous.

If we're honest, offended people are unwilling and sometimes just too lazy to do the hard work of putting forth the necessary energy and effort needed to forgive and love. Many of them are simply too weak to do what's right. Zero Victim thinkers don't initially try to change people and circumstances. They first change what they think and feel about them, and subsequently how they respond to them.

As a Zero Victim thinker, I have learned to manage people circles in my head. I'm constantly shifting people and my thoughts about them in and out of different circles in my head concerning what I think and expect from them. By doing so, I never allow them to offend me because I've placed them in the right circle.

People can only offend you when you place them in the wrong circle. I don't demand that people adjust to me. I adjust to them by making a Zero Victim mental adjustment and placing them in the right circle in my mind.

Speak Peace to the Storm

Jesus lived in a place of such inner peace, when confronted by a raging storm, He spoke to the storm out of His own internal peaceful nature to subdue it.

> *But He was in the stern, asleep on a pillow. And they awoke Him and said to Him, "Teacher, do You not care that we are perishing?" Then He arose and rebuked the wind, and said to the sea, "Peace, be still!" And the wind ceased and there was a great calm. But He said to them, "Why are you so fearful? How is it that you have no faith?" And they feared exceedingly, and said to one another, "Who can this be, that even the wind and the sea obey Him!"* (Mark 4:38-41 NKJV)

The calm inside Jesus was greater than the storm around Him. He didn't call peace down from Heaven, peace was inside Him. Although Jesus was in the storm, He didn't let the storm get in Him, and neither should we.

This book explains many practical things we can do to develop Zero Victim thinking, but ultimately, the true solution to eliminating victimization is being *born again* and becoming a true follower of the God of love and His Son Jesus Christ.

Through faith in Christ, you are now empowered by God. As you continue to live by faith, you will never again live as a victim of the circumstances of life. Once you bow your knee to Jesus, you will never have to bow to anything or anyone else in life, because you are not a victim! As you grow spiritually, God will increasingly renew your mind, causing you to think more and more like Him. He will assist you in being completely free from the mentality of defeat. On to your victory my friend! On to your victory! Be encouraged!

"The calm inside Jesus was greater than the storm around Him."

ABOUT THE AUTHOR

James Ward is a pastor, author, visionary, and entrepreneur who has emerged as an international, conscionable voice of spiritual and moral authority. Because of his unique Zero Victim, Biblical perspective, his involvement is highly sought after by corporate, government, and thought leaders, in mitigating the complex challenges surrounding racial and socio-political issues. He is known for his keen insight into the social complexities of spirituality and intersectionality.

As a speaker, James emphasizes Christian character and leadership development, while intellectually challenging listeners with proven wisdom based upon Biblical principles. He is a strategist and advocate for holistic social healing, renewal, reconciliation, and transformation.

The Zero Victim principles in this book have fueled James' success in every area of life. He is pastor and founder of INSIGHT Church in the north Chicago suburb of Skokie. He and his wife Sharon have been married for twenty-one years and have two wonderful children, Hannah and Jonathan.

Website: www.jamesewardjr.com
Email: info@jw-mi.org
Facebook: jamesewardjr
Instagram: @jamesewardjr
Twitter: @jamesewardjr

Printed in the USA
CPSIA information can be obtained
at www.ICGtesting.com
CBHW031033250923
1126CB00001B/1